Perl Debugger
Pocket Reference

Richard Foley

Beijing · Cambridge · Farnham · Köln · Paris · Sebastopol · Taipei · Tokyo

Perl Debugger Pocket Reference
by Richard Foley

Published by O'Reilly & Associates, Inc., 1005 Gravenstein Highway North, Sebastopol, CA 95472.

O'Reilly & Associates books may be purchased for educational, business, or sales promotional use. Online editions are also available for most titles (*safari.oreilly.com*). For more information, contact our corporate/institutional sales department: (800) 998-9938 or *corporate@oreilly.com*.

Editor:	Linda Mui
Production Editor:	Sarah Sherman
Cover Designer:	Emma Colby
Interior Designer:	David Futato

Printing History:

January 2004:	First Edition.

0-596-00503-2
[C]

Contents

Perl Debugger
Pocket Reference

What Is the Perl Debugger?

In the ideal world, every program would be perfect the first
time it is written. In reality, however, even the best programmers make mistakes or forget to provide for all situations.

The Perl debugger is an application you can use to follow the
logic of a Perl program while it is being executed, saving you
time and frustration in tracking down bugs in your programs.
With the Perl debugger, you can stop the program at selected
points, print and modify the contents of variables, and print
stack traces out to see what has been called from where.

This book describes every command, option, and variable of
the Perl debugger. Any intermediate to advanced Perl programmer should be familiar with the debugger to save time
and frustration while debugging their programs.

Why Use the Debugger?

There are many ways to find out what is going wrong in a Perl
program. Reading through the code with a co-programmer,
for example, often helps bring revelations to light. The hum-
ble print statement itself has probably saved more programs
than there are programmers; simply inserting print statements at strategic points in the program can reveal surprising
behavior that often leads to the discovery of logical lapses.

Sometimes, however, there comes a time when the simple print statement is not enough. You might need to diagnose a problem on a program already in production that you are unable to modify. In this case, it is invaluable to be able to run the program, stop it wherever you wish, and check or perhaps modify the internal state of certain data structures without modifying the program itself.

Even when you can modify the program, scattering print statements all over the place is generally unhealthy. For example, you might insert an extra next or last statement into a loop that is accidentally forgotten, changing the program logic. The harder the problem is, the more risk of disruptions to the code, as more and more allegedly harmless code modifications are inserted.

The beauty of the debugger is that the running behavior of the application can be inspected and modified without changing any of the code. The Perl debugger gives you this control; the print statement does not.

Unfamiliar Territory

People shy away from using the debugger for several reasons. Many are awed by the slightly heavy looking documentation, which is both scattered and, in places, vague or incomplete. This book remedies this situation by bringing everything into a single, small, and easy-to-use reference volume.

Also, in today's multiskilled world, programmers are very often people who have cross-trained into the sector without having formally studied the subject. Many programmers working today have never been taught the basic functional use of a debugger in a computer-science class. Many programmers are therefore unfamiliar with actually stepping through their program, one executable statement at a time, to investigate the actual value of variables at runtime, and to change the behavior of the program without modifying the code.

Once you have discovered this ability, it is a marvelous thing to use. Even when a program is working perfectly, stepping through it in the debugger is oftentimes the best way to get to know the working behavior of an inherited program.

Finally, an often quoted declaration is that "Larry favors the print statement."[*] I can only reply (in addition to the comments above) that if I were Larry I'm sure I wouldn't need to debug nearly so much in the first place. However, because I'm not Larry, I'll use any tool at my disposal to make debugging my program easier and faster, including the debugger, which he also wrote.

In my experience, the debugger is a greatly underused tool. When I ask even hard-core Perl developers, only about 30% of them have actually used it. If this reference helps to redress the balance a bit, and more people put the debugger in their troubleshooting toolkit, this book will have done its job.

About This Book

The debugger commands in this book are grouped by the type of behavior, increasing in level of complexity. I show the syntax for every command or option, and an example of each argument variation. At the end of this book is a quick reference with simple summaries of each command.

The code I use to demonstrate the commands is fundamentally clean working code, which at first sight might seem a bit odd in a book describing a tool that can help in solving problem code. The rationale is that rather than find a new problem for each command to demonstrate how clever I am in finding new problems, I have decided to concentrate on explaining the commands and their operation in a fully operational environment. Engineers study working models to discover how materials and design solutions might work

[*] Larry Wall, inventor of Perl, in case you picked up the wrong book by accident.

together to prevent problems. They do not make a habit of studying only broken bridges when it is too late to fix them.

You are encouraged to try the examples in this book at any point throughout this book. Completing a task is a far better way of learning than just reading about it.

When you need to get into the debugger without a program, use the following syntax:

```
perldb@monkey> perl -d -e 0
```

which supplies 0 to the debugger as the (bogus) command-line program to execute.

The linecounter.pl Script

When we need to step through an existing program in this book, I refer mostly to a program I call *linecounter.pl*, which reports which lines in a file match a given pattern. It is a reasonable demonstration script, because it has command-line arguments, uses a module, includes a loop, calls a subroutine, etc. For the purposes of this book, I usually call it something like this:

```
perldb@monkey> perl -d linecounter.pl pattern inputfile
```

This and any other code used in this book can be found on the O'Reilly website at:

http://www.oreilly.com/the-perl-debugger/code

If you're reading this book on top of a mountain and don't have online access, here is the source code with comments removed for brevity:

```
use strict;
use FileHandle;

my @args = @ARGV;

my $help = grep(/^-h[elp]*$/i, @args);
if ($help) {
  print logg(help());
  exit 0;
}
```

```perl
my $verbose = grep(/^-v[erbose]*$/i, @args);

my $REGEX = shift @args || '';

my @files = grep(!/^-(h[elp]*|v[erbose]*)$/i, @args);
unless (@files) {
  push(@files, $0);
  logg("using default $0 while no files given");
}

foreach my $file (@files) {
  if (-f $file && -r _) {
    my $FH = FileHandle->new("< $file");
    if ($FH) {
      logg("file($file)");
      my %report = %{report($FH, $REGEX)}; # -> subroutine
      if (keys %report) {
        logg("the LINENO and CHARACTERS matching the
pattern($REGEX) for '$file': ");
        foreach my $len (sort { $a <=> $b } keys %report) {
          print "    ".sprintf("%-10.d", $len)."
$report{$len}\n";
        }
      } else {
        logg("no matching pattern($REGEX) found in '$file'");
      }
    } else {
      error("failed to open file($file) $!");
    }
  } else {
    error("no such or unreadable file($file) $!");
  }
}

sub report {
  my $FH = shift;
  my $regex = shift;
  my %report = ();
  my $i_cnt = 0;
  while (<$FH>) {
    $i_cnt++;
    my $i_match = 0;
    my $line = $_;
    if ($line =~ /($regex)/) {
      $report{$i_cnt} = $1; #
      $i_match++;
    } else {
      $i_match = 0;
    }
    logg("\t[$i_cnt] regex($regex) matched($i_match)
      <-$line");
```

```
      }
      $FH->close;
      return \%report;
    }

    exit 0;

    sub help {
      return  qq|Usage: $0 pattern file [file]+ [-help]
          [-verbose]|."\n".
          qq|Example: perl $0 \^\.*\\s*mat input_file|
      ;
    }

    sub logg {
      my $msg = join("\n", @_)."\n";
      print STDOUT $msg if $verbose;
      return $msg;
    }

    sub error {
      my $error = shift;
      logg("Error: $error", @_);
    }
```

Shell

Throughout this book I use the bash shell on Linux. Certain commands may need to be adapted if you are using a different shell on a different platform. For example, when exporting a variable into the environment, I typically do it in the bash shell like this:

```
perldb@monkey> VAR_NAME=var_value perl -d program args
```

which exports the VAR_NAME variable into my environment with the value var_value for the duration of that program call. Your mileage may vary with your shell and operating system.

Truncated Output

Note that the debugger is somewhat verbose in its output, so I have truncated most of its output in order to save space. Empty lines have unceremoniously been removed. Snipped text is indicated with the <...truncated output...> marker,

---

used for verbose code or variable listings where the amount of peripheral noise would dilute the demonstration.

Also, where the output of some commands runs off the right-hand side of the page, and where this output is not deemed relevant to the example, I have trimmed the offending text and indicated this with the ... marker.

Versions of Perl

This book uses the Perl 5.8.0 distribution, spearheaded by Jarkko Hietenami and the *perl5-porters* (running on Linux). While there have been changes to certain commands from earlier versions, and those changes are mentioned where relevant, the command set described in this book applies to most historical versions of *perl5db.pl* with minimal changes. Before you do anything else, you should browse the existing *perldoc*s; the most important are mentioned in the text as needed.

Delving Deeper

This book concentrates on debugging programs written in Perl using the debugger as supplied in a standard Perl distribution. Getting at the internals of Perl (written in C) would require the use of a C source-level debugger such as *gdb* and is outside the scope of this book. If you are interested in debugging Perl itself, you should familarize yourself with the *perlguts*, *perlapi*, *perlcall*, and *perlhack* manpages.

Conventions

Constant width is used to indicate code, function names, and anything to be typed literally.

Constant bold is used to indicate user input.

Italics are used for program names.

Constant *italics* are used to show comments in the code listings.

Acknowledgments and Disclaimers

Thanks to my family—Joy, Catherine, Jennifer, and Spot the dog—for being so patient while this book was being written. Thanks also to the reviewers—Ronald Kimball, Joe McMahon, Nicholas Clark, and Gabor Szabo—who through their feedback have produced a much better book. Thanks to my editor at O'Reilly, Linda Mui, without whom this book would surely never have seen the light of day.

Although I have tried to be thorough and the reviewers did a great job, it is always possible that I may have missed something. I take full responsibility for any errors which may remain.

Before You Debug

Before running the debugger, there are a number of things you can do that will make debugging more straightforward. If you restrict the number of poor programming habits that are currently reflected in the code, you may find that you don't need the debugger at all. Sometimes just talking through the execution of your application with a fellow programmer may be all it takes to clarify what's wrong with the logic.

Some of the following tools and suggestions may also prove useful. If these aren't already part of your programming arsenal, they should be.

Check Your Syntax

Perhaps the first thing to do with any program is to check it for syntax flaws without actually running it. The -c switch loads the Perl program, compiles it, and checks it for syntax errors:

```
perldb@monkey> perl -c prog
program syntax OK
```

Note that Perl executes any BEGIN and CHECK blocks, as well as any use statements, as these are considered compile-time code.

Perl does not run any require statements or INIT blocks. require statements are runtime code and are not executed during the syntax check.

perl -c is especially useful when editing a file in a programmer's text editor, where it is possible to syntax check the current program being edited. For example, in vi's command-line mode, you can check that your code is Perl compliant with the following line:

```
:!perl -cWT %
```

Use strict

The strict pragma disallows soft references, ensures that all variables are declared before usage, and disallows barewords except for subroutines.

Once a program has been written, making it strict-compliant is notoriously awkward, particularly when your program (written by a predecessor; not you, of course!) may have reused certain variables in a different scope and possibly made use of global variables with abandon. I have seen some installations where a single subroutine spanning several hundred lines reused the same variable name in multiple nested loops, which is a disaster waiting to happen.

One of the powerful things about Perl is that strict mode is optional. Nevertheless, most people should enable it. It is much simpler to put use strict in *before* you start writing code, if only for a quieter life afterwards.

Consider the following code in a file called *variable.pl*, which has strict enabled and includes a compile-time error:

```
$variable = 'auto-declared';   # ok
use strict;
$variable = 'second use';      # this is a compile time error
my $variable = 'now ok';       # ok
print "$variable\n";
```

Now run the code:

```
perldb@monkey> perl ./variable.pl
Variable "$variable" is not imported at ./variable.pl line 3.
Global symbol "$variable" requires explicit package name at ./
variable.pl line 3.
Execution of ./variable.pl aborted due to compilation errors.
```

Because strict is in effect, the program is aborted. If use strict had been omitted, the program would have run without a complaint.

Note that strict can be turned off selectively for a block of code:

```
use strict;
{
    no strict;
    $variable = 'never seen before';  # no strict effect
}
# $variable = 'strict in this scope'; # compile time error
my $variable = 'now ok';              # ok
print "$variable\n";
```

Now run the code:

```
perldb@monkey> perl ./variable.pl
now ok
```

For more information, see the documentation for *strict*.

Establish a Good
Development Environment

One frequent problem is the lack of a sensible developer environment to help programmers work together on concurrent versions of an application. When a number of people are developing or fixing each other's code, it is imperative to use a source code versioning system, like *cvs*, and to have an automatic testing system in place. By running the test suite automatically after any changes have been applied, you ensure that nothing has been broken, reducing the amount of debugging required in the first place.

For more information on *diff*, *patch* and *cvs*, see their respective manpages. For a test module, see Test::More.

Warnings

Turning warnings on causes Perl to emit warning messages about code constructs it considers dubious under certain conditions. You can turn warnings on for the entire program with the -w command-line switch. To turn on warnings locally (that is, only within a discrete block of code), you can enable use warnings or use the special variable $^W.

For example, consider *print.pl*, a program containing only the following line:

```
print $ARGV[0];
```

If you use the -w switch, expect the following output:

```
perldb@monkey> perl -w print.pl
Use of uninitialized value in print at program line 1 (#1)
```

If you want to turn warnings off for the entire program, use the -X command-line switch. To turn off warnings locally, use no warnings or set $^W=0, which overrides all locally set flags.

If you want to turn all warnings on, use -W. Warnings are set regardless of locally-set $^W=0 and no warnings declarations.

For more information, see the *perllexwarn* and *warnings* manpages.

Diagnostics

If Perl's error and warning messages do not provide enough information, use the diagnostics pragma. With the *print.pl* program shown previously, add diagnostics output by hard-wiring the pragma within the program:

```
use diagnostics;
print $ARGV[0];
```

Now the program emits verbose diagnostic messages:

```
perldb@monkey> perl ./print.pl
Use of uninitialized value in print at warning line 1 (#1)
```

```
(W uninitialized) An undefined value was used as if it were
already defined.  It was interpreted as a "" or a 0, but maybe
it was a mistake.
To suppress this warning assign a defined value to your
variables.

To help you figure out what was undefined, Perl tells you what
operation you used the undefined value in.  Note, however,
that Perl optimizes your program and the operation displayed
in the warning may not necessarily appear literally in your
program.  For text, "that $foo" is usually optimized into
"that " . $foo, and the warning will refer to the
concatenation (.) operator, even though there is no . in your
program.
```

If you don't want to hardwire the use diagnostics statement directly into your code, you can get the same behavior by using the -M command-line switch:

```
perldb@monkey> perl -Mdiagnostics -w print.pl
Use of uninitialized value in print at warning line 1 (#1)
(W uninitialized) An undefined value was used as if it were
<...truncated output...>
```

Note that this diagnostic information is generated via *perldiag*. It is equally valid to look up the messages directly in the Perl manpages.

If you think you have discovered a bug in Perl, it's a good idea to run your program with use diagnostics enabled before you report the bug. Sometimes this helps to clarify otherwise inexplicable behavior and saves the trouble of generating an erroneous bug report. You might also check for known bugs at the Perl bug database.

For more information on diagnostics, see the *perldiag* and *splain* manpages.

Taint Mode

Tainting is a kind of paranoid mechanism in which Perl treats every variable from outside your program as "tainted," or dangerous, and refuses to run external programs from unacknowledged locations. You enable taint mode from the command line with the -T command-line option.

The splain Program

The *splain* program accepts warning messages and converts them to verbose messages, precisely as use diagnostics does, but again with the advantage of not having to hardwire anything into the code. Any time you have a message you don't understand, give *splain* a chance to decipher it on your behalf:

```
perldb@monkey> perl -w print.pl | splain
Use of uninitialized value in print at warning line 1
(W uninitialized) An undefined value was used as if it
<...truncated output...>
```

For more information, see the manpage for *splain*.

When you pass the -T flag to Perl, it enables certain checks to prevent the careless programmer from shooting herself in the foot. It forces her to check, or *untaint*, each external chunk of data before being allowed to use it. Any process running on behalf of other users, such as CGI programs that normally run under a special web server account, should have taint enabled.

Sometimes you have to jump through various hoops to get your program to work smoothly with taint enabled, but it is invariably worth it. In the following example (in a program called *taint.pl*), an external program (*/bin/echo*) is called, where the directory in which it resides (*/bin/*) is not in the environment $PATH:

```
#!/usr/bin/perl -T

# $ENV{PATH}='/bin';
system "/bin/echo Hello World";
```

Perl rightfully complains when this program is run:

```
perldb@monkey> ./taint.pl
Insecure $ENV{PATH} while running with -T switch at taint.pl
line 1.
```

Uncomment the $ENV{PATH}='/bin'; line, and Perl allows the program to call the executable (presuming the path is correct) and prints the expected line:

```
perldb@monkey> ./taint.pl
Hello World
```

Perl doesn't like to take any chances with taint mode, so it insists that taint be enabled at the command line. There's no use taint, special variable, or any other mechanism for turning taint mode on and off in the middle of the program; taint mode must be turned at the command line or not at all. This means that if you need to call Perl directly on the command line (perhaps you want to use a particular version of Perl, or you are passing other command-line switches such as -d for the debugger), Perl will complain about it being too late for the taint switch, even if it appears on the #! line at the very top of the program. Even the first line of a program is considered "too late":

```
perldb@monkey> perl ./taint.pl
Too late for "-T" option at ./taint.pl line 1.
```

The solution is simple: just place -T as a command-line option, so Perl can see it early enough:

```
perldb@monkey> perl -T ./taint.pl
Hello World
```

If you need something a bit lighter, you can use -t (introduced in 5.8.0), which enables taint in a warnings-only mode. While the standard behavior with -T is to treat failing constructs as fatal errors, the -t option allows the program to still run, emitting only warnings:

```
perldb@monkey> perl -t ./taint.pl
Insecure $ENV{PATH} while running with -t switch at ./program
line 3.
Insecure directory in $ENV{PATH} while running with -t switch
at ./program line 3.
Insecure dependency in system while running with -t switch at
./program line 3.
Hello World
```

The -t option overrides later -T switches.

For more information on taint mode, see the *Taint* and *perlsec* manpages.

A Debugger Tutorial

In this section I present a couple of very short sessions to demonstrate some simple debugger usage. I show a simple debugger session with no program and then a walkthrough of debugging a CGI program with a couple of problems.

Starting a Session

For an example of its simplest usage, start the debugger by giving it something innocuous as the evaluation argument to the debugger via the command line. I like to use a 0 (zero) as the evaluation argument as my entry to the debugger. Use the -d option to call the debugger and the -e 0 option to specify 0 as the evaluation script:

```
perldb@monkey> perl -d -e 0
Default die handler restored.

Loading DB routines from perl5db.pl version 1.19
Editor support available.

Enter h or 'h h' for help, or 'man perldebug' for more help.

main::(-e:1):   0
  DB<1>
```

Perl stops at the first executable statement, which in this example is 0, a perfectly valid (though minimal) Perl expression. If you continue now, you'll just fall off the end of the program.

Although this example may not immediately appear to be very useful, at this point you can in fact interact completely with the debugger. You can look at any environment variables (V) and you can also check out the help (h) page/s, and explore your surroundings.

To get the help page simply type h at the command prompt:

```
DB<1> h
```

List/search source lines:		Control script execution:	
l [ln|sub]	List source code	T	Stack trace
- or .	List previous/current line	s [expr]	Single step [in expr]
w [line]	List around line	n [expr]	Next, steps over subs
f filename	View source in file	<CR/Enter>	Repeat last n or s
/pattern/ ?patt?	Search forw/backw	r	Return from subroutine
v	Show versions of modules	c [ln|sub]	Continue until position
Debugger controls:		L	List break/watch/actions
O [...]	Set debugger options	t [expr]	Toggle trace [trace expr]
<[<]{[{]}>[>]		b [ln|event|	
[cmd]	Do pre/post-prompt	sub] [cnd]	Set breakpoint
! [N|pat]	Redo a previous command	d [ln] or D	Delete a/all breakpoints
H [-num]	Display last num commands	a [ln] cmd	Do cmd before line
= [a val]	Define/list an alias	W expr	Add a watch expression
h [db_cmd]	Get help on command	A or W	Delete all actions/watch
|[|]db_cmd	Send output to pager	!![!] syscmd	Run cmd in a subprocess
q or ^D	Quit	R	Attempt a restart
Data Examination:		expr	Execute perl code, also see: s,n,t
expr			
x|m expr	Evals expr in list context, dumps the result or lists methods.		
p expr	Print expression (uses script's current package).		
S [[!]pat]	List subroutine names [not] matching pattern		
V [Pk [Vars]]	List Variables in Package. Vars can be ~pattern or !pattern.		
X [Vars]	Same as "V current_package [Vars]".		

For more help, type h cmd_letter, or run man perldebug for all docs.

```
DB<2>
```

You can run any Perl code you like in this environment. You can think of it as a form of Perl shell. For example, suppose you can't remember whether the results of a regular expression are given in scalar or array context. Instead of looking it up in *perlre*, try it in the debugger. First create a string $str:

```
DB<2> $str = 'some string'
DB<3>
```

Then print $str with the debugger's p command, which is just Perl's print command in disguise:

```
DB<3> p $str
some string
DB<4>
```

Now capture the return value of a regex into a scalar named $res and print the result:

```
DB<4> $res = $str =~ /(\w+)\s+(\w+)/
DB<5> p $res
1
  DB<6>
```

From this result, you should see that a regex doesn't assign a meaningful value to a scalar. Now capture the return value of the same regex into an array variable named @res and print that:

```
DB<7> @res = $str =~ /(\w+)\s+(\w+)/
DB<8> p @res
somestring
  DB<9>
```

From this little experiment, you should have discovered that regexes return their results in an array context. Use x to dump the results to get a clearer picture:

```
DB<9> x \@res
0   ARRAY(0x844df5c)
   0  'some'
   1  'string'
   DB<10>
```

In a similar fashion, see what happens when you increment a string, a strange but possibly useful thing to want to do. In any event, it is harmless enough to try it. First create and print a string variable:

```
DB<10> $foo = 'abc'
DB<11> p $foo
abc
  DB<12>
```

Increment the string and print the result:

```
DB<12> ++$foo
DB<13> p $foo
abd
  DB<14>
```

So incrementing a string ends up incrementing the last character in the string.

At this point, you haven't loaded any program to debug, but you should have a feel of how to move around inside the debugger. You can continue to play around in the debugger to your heart's content now. To exit a debugger session, use the q command:

```
DB<14> q
perldb@monkey>
```

A Simple CGI Debugger Session

For this session you will use an actual program, with actual problems. First copy this code, which can be downloaded from the O'Reilly website, into a file called *problem.cgi*:

```
use CGI;
my $o_cgi = new CGI();

my %data = (
  name    => $o_cgi->param('Name')    || 'UNKNOWN',
  company => $o_cgi->param('company') || 'UNKNOWN',
);

$data{name} =~ s/^(.)?(.+)$/uc($1);lc($2)/e;

print $o_cgi->header(-type=>'text/html'),
     $o_cgi->start_html(-title=>'Perl Debugger Tutorial'),
     qq|
  <hr>
  Hi <b>$data{name}</b> welcome to the <i>$data{company}</i>
debugger home page!
  <hr>
|,    $o_cgi->end_html."\n";

exit 0;
```

Now call it on the command line with name and company arguments to view the output:

```
perldb@monkey> perl problem.cgi name=monkey company=Perl
Content-Type: text/html; charset=ISO-8859-1

<?xml version="1.0" encoding="iso-8859-1"?>
<!DOCTYPE html
    PUBLIC "-//W3C//DTD XHTML 1.0 Transitional//EN"
    "http://www.w3.org/TR/xhtml1/DTD/xhtml1-transitional.dtd">
<html xmlns="http://www.w3.org/1999/xhtml" lang="en-US"><head>
<title>Perl Debugger Tutorial</title>
```

```
</head><body>
    <hr>
    Hi <b>nknown</b> - welcome to the Perl debugger home page!
    <hr>
</body></html>
perldb@monkey>
```

The program prints vast amounts of Web-centric information that is irrelevant to us. More importantly, a user with a
name of monkey has been welcomed with the impressively
wrong:

```
Hi <b>nknown</b> - welcome to the Perl debugger home page!
```

Instead of monkey, the program thinks the user is called
nknown.

There are several ways to approach this problem. Running
the program with warnings or diagnostics would certainly
help locate some problems. You can also try to make sense of
it via the debugger. Run the same command again, this time
with the -d option:

```
perldb@monkey> perl -d problem.cgi name=monkey company=Perl
<...truncated output...>
main::(problem.cgi:2):  my $o_cgi = new CGI();
  DB<1>
```

The program has stopped execution at the first executable
line and is waiting for an instruction. Get a code listing to see
where you are; use the l command for a code listing:

```
  DB<1>l
2==>    my $o_cgi = new CGI();
3
4:      my %data = (
5           name    => $o_cgi->param('Name')    || 'UNKNOWN',
6           company => $o_cgi->param('company') || 'UNKNOWN',
7       );
8
9:      $data{name} =~ s/^(.)?(.+)$/uc($1);lc($2)/e;
10
11:     print $o_cgi->header(-type=>'text/html'),
  DB<1>
```

Although you have not executed anything yet, print out the command line using p to confirm that the program has really been given the correct arguments:

```
DB<1> p "args: @ARGV"
args: name=monkey company=Perl
DB<2>
```

This looks good. Now use n to step over the first executable statement, which enables CGI to pick up the user input:

```
DB<2> n
main::(./problem.cgi:4):        my %data = (
main::(./problem.cgi:5):                    name    => $o_cgi->
param('Name')    || 'UNKNOWN',
main::(./problem.cgi:6):                    company => $o_cgi->
param('company') || 'UNKNOWN',
main::(./problem.cgi:7):        );
DB<2>
```

This shows that Perl considers the next 4 lines of code as a single command to execute within the current scope. Notice that you are about to be given an invalid parameter by using Name, instead of the name that you used on the command line.

Check this by printing the value returned by $o_cgi-> param('Name'):

```
DB<2> p $o_cgi->param('Name')

DB<3>
```

After making a note to modify line 5 with the appropriate name argument in the source code at a later stage, adjust the current value for the CGI object directly, printing it to make sure it is correct:

```
DB<3> p $o_cgi->param('Name', 'monkey')
monkey
DB<4>
```

Use n to step to the next executable statement:

```
DB<4> n
main::(./problem.cgi:9):        $data{name} =~ s/^(.)?(.+)$/
uc($1);lc($2)/e;
DB<4>
```

Use x to print out the contents of the %data structure. Note the use of a reference, which tells the debugger to "pretty print" the dumped data:

```
  DB<4> x \%data
0  HASH(0x817e758)
   'company' => 'Perl'
   'name' => 'monkey'
  DB<5>
```

This explains why the parameter appears as unknown, but not why it appears as nknown. The first character of the user's name has been lost. Use c 11 to continue to line 11 and check the $data{name} again:

```
  DB<5> c 11
main::(./problem.cgi:11):    print $o_cgi->header(-type=>'text/
html'),
main::(./problem.cgi:12):              $o_cgi->start_html(-
title=>'Perl Debugger Tutorial'),
main::(./problem.cgi:13):              qq|
main::(./problem.cgi:14):              <hr>
main::(./problem.cgi:15):              Hi <b>$data{name}</b>
welcome to the <i>$data{company}</i> debugger home page!
main::(./problem.cgi:16):              <hr>
main::(./problem.cgi:17):      |,   $o_cgi->end_html."\n";
  DB<6> p $data{name}
onkey
  DB<7>
```

Clearly, something is not right: the name monkey has its first character stripped and appears as onkey. If you look at line 9, you can see that uc( ) is used on the first and single character and lc( ) on the remainder of monkey, which looks suspiciously like the source of the problem:

```
  DB<7> l 9
9==>    $data{name} =~ s/^(.)?(.+)$/uc($1);lc($2)/e;
  DB<8>
```

First, check the value of the current matches:

```
  DB<8> p $1
m
  DB<9> p $2
onkey
  DB<10>
```

These look good, but a closer look at the expression reveals that /uc($1);lc($2)/ produces two values when you are only assigning to one.

Try resetting the $data{name} and running a version of line 11 that concatenates the matches, by replacing the ; with a ., and see what happens:

```
DB<10> $data{name} =~ s/^(.)?(.+)$/uc($1).lc($2)/e
DB<11> p $data{name}
Monkey
DB<12>
```

That's it! Fix the source code, rerun the code to check that the output looks like the following line, and you're done:

```
Hi <b>Monkey</b> welcome to the <i>Perl</i> debugger home
page!
```

For an extensive tutorial introduction to the Perl debugger, see *perldebtut*, the debugger tutorial provided with Perl. For CGI-specific debugging see the *CGI*, *cgidebug*, and *perlfaq9* manpages.

Debugger Commands

In this section, I go over each of the commands in the debugger, grouped into logical topic areas, as shown in Table 1.

Table 1. Debugger command groupings

Topic area	Commands covered
Help and quitting	h, q, man
Examining data	m, M, p, S, V, x, X, y
Listing code and searching	l, v, ., -, //, ??, f
Motion	c, n, s, r, T, t
Actions, breakpoints, and watchpoints	a, b, w, L
Perl, pre-prompt, and post-prompt commands	<, >, <<, >>, {, {{
Shell, setting options, and debugger commands	o, |, ||, !!, .perldb, source, H, !, R, =

Also refer to the quick-reference to the debugger commands at the end of the book.

From here on in, assume that you are in a debugger session. For your current purposes, you don't even need a proper program to start a session. Just type perl -d -e 0 at the command line, which drops you into a debugger session and waits for an instruction to execute:

```
perldb@monkey> perl -d -e 0
<...truncated output...>
main::(-e:1):   0
  DB<1>
```

Help and Quitting

When learning a new skill, the first thing to learn is what to do when you get stuck. So before you get in too deep with the debugger, it's important to learn how to get help and how to quit. This section covers:

- How to find both quick and detailed help
- How to access the built-in Perl documentation library (a.k.a. *perldoc*) as well as the system manpages
- How to quit the debugger session

---

h   The basic help command

h [cmd]

Produces a screen of information briefly describing all available debugger commands:

```
    DB<1> h
List/search source lines:               Control script execution:
  l [ln|sub]    List source code          T           Stack trace
  - or .        List previous/current line s [expr]    Single step [in expr]
  w [line]      List around line          n [expr]    Next, steps over subs
  f filename    View source in file       <CR/Enter>  Repeat last n or s
  /pattern/ ?patt? Search forw/backw      r           Return from subroutine
  v             Show versions of modules  c [ln|sub]  Continue until position
Debugger controls:                        L           List break/watch/actions
  O [...]       Set debugger options      t [expr]    Toggle trace [trace expr]
  <[<]|{[{]|>[>]                          b [ln|event|
    [cmd]       Do pre/post-prompt          sub] [cnd] Set breakpoint
```

Command	Description	Command	Description
! [N|pat]	Redo a previous command	d [ln] or D	Delete a/all breakpoints
H [-num]	Display last num commands	a [ln] cmd	Do cmd before line
= [a val]	Define/list an alias	W expr	Add a watch expression
h [db_cmd]	Get help on command	A or W	Delete all actions/watch
|[|]db_cmd	Send output to pager	![!] syscmd	Run cmd in a subprocess
q or ^D	Quit	R	Attempt a restart
Data Examination:		expr	Execute perl code, also see: s,n,t

```
expr
x|m expr       Evals expr in list context, dumps the result or lists methods.
p expr         Print expression (uses script's current package).
S [[!]pat]     List subroutine names [not] matching pattern
V [Pk [Vars]]  List Variables in Package. Vars can be ~pattern or !pattern.
X [Vars]       Same as "V current_package [Vars]".
For more help, type h cmd_letter, or run man perldebug for all docs.
  DB<1>
```

To view the help for a particular command, give the command name as an argument:

```
DB<1> h n
n [expr]       Next, steps over subroutine calls [in expr].
DB<2>
```

Note that the h and h h commands are swapped in versions of Perl prior to 5.8.0.

---

h h   Extended help

h h

Gives extended help by printing information for all available commands.

Because this command generates particularly long output, the best way to view it is to pipe it through your pager by using |h h so you can read all of it on one screen. See the later section "Shell and Debugger Commands" for more information on the | command:

```
perldb@monkey> perl -d -e 0
<...truncated output...>
main::(-e:1):   0
  DB<1> h h
Help is currently only available for the new 580 CommandSet,
if you really want old behaviour, presumably you know what
you're doing ?-)
T               Stack trace.
s [expr]        Single step [in expr].
n [expr]        Next, steps over subroutine calls [in expr].
<CR>            Repeat last n or s command.
r               Return from current subroutine.
```

```
c [line|sub]     Continue; optionally inserts a one-time-only
                 break point at the specified position.
l min+incr       List incr+1 lines starting at min.
l min-max        List lines min through max.

<...truncated output...>

h [db_command]   Get help [on a specific debugger command], enter
                 |h to page.
h h              Long help for debugger commands
man manpage      Runs the external doc viewer man command on the
                 named Perl manpage, or on man itself if omitted.
                 Set $DB::doccmd to change viewer.
Type '|h h' for a paged display if this was too hard to read.
  DB<2>
```

Note that the h and h h commands are swapped in versions of Perl
prior to 5.8.0.

---

man   The manpage wrapper

man *manpage*

Runs the $DB::doccmd command on the given argument. For
example, to view the documentation on predefined Perl variables
in the middle of a session, type the following command:

```
    DB<3> man perlvar
PERLVAR(1)        Perl Programmers Reference Guide
PERLVAR(1)

NAME
    perlvar - Perl predefined variables

DESCRIPTION
    Predefined Names

    The following names have special meaning to Perl.

<...truncated output...>
  DB<4>
```

Because the debugger environment is so helpful, you could even
leave "perl" off, and it would be prepended for you:

```
    DB<3> man var
```

You could just as easily use perldoc perlvar, but man var is less to
type.

To change the documentation viewer, see the section "Quick
Reference" later in this book.

---

q

To quit the current debug session, type q or ^D. You should get
your shell prompt back.

```
    DB<4> q
  perldb@monkey>
```

Examining Data

This section covers the commands available to print and
examine variables and data structures. They cover:

- How to find out what methods or functions are available
- How to print out simple data structures and dump complicated ones
- What variables exist in the current package or any other
  package that is currently loaded

The following commands enable you to examine almost anything in a running Perl program, from simple scalar variables
to deeply nested hashes and objects to callable methods.
Each of these commands print out to varying depths or level
of detail, the contents of the expression given as an argument.

---

p   Print an expression

p *expr*

The p command is just a wrapper for the standard Perl print statement. It prints the given expression in the current package. The
output is printed to the filehandle given by $DB::OUT (see the
section entitled "Debugger Variables").

Note that the p command just prints the stringified value; it does
not dump the expression. If you want a complex data structure
dump, see the x command later in this section:

```
  perldb@monkey> perl -d -e 0
  <...truncated output...>
    DB<1> $foo = 123
    DB<2> p $foo
```

```
123
  DB<3> p ++$foo
124
  DB<4> p qw(one two three)
onetwothree
  DB<5> $bar = bless({foo=$foo},'Foo')>
  DB<6> p $bar
Foo=HASH(0x828e97c)
```

---

m

m (*expr*|*class*)

Lists the methods that can be called on the given expression or class.

Given an expression (m *expr*), this command evaluates the expression in a list context and returns methods, or subroutines, that can be called against the first element of the result. For example:

```
perldb@monkey> perl -d -e 0
<...truncated output...>
  DB<1> $fh = FileHandle->new('> /tmp/xxx')
  DB<2> m $fh
DESTROY
_IOFBF
_IOLBF
_IONBF
_open_mode_string
autoflush
clearerr
close
<...truncated output...>
via UNIVERSAL: VERSION
via UNIVERSAL: can
via UNIVERSAL: isa
  DB<3>
```

This command cannot apply to methods that have not been created at runtime. For example, it cannot apply where AUTOLOAD is used to generate methods on the fly, because the methods cannot be known in advance.

Note also that all packages include at least the last three methods discussed, inherited via the built-in UNIVERSAL package Perl provides. To demonstrate this, build a vanilla package:

```
  DB<3> package Mine;
  DB<4> m Mine
via UNIVERSAL: VERSION
via UNIVERSAL: can
via UNIVERSAL: isa
  DB<5>
```

Now add some of your own methods and display these:

```
DB<5> package Mine; sub new {}; sub first {};
DB<6> m Mine
first
new
via UNIVERSAL: VERSION
via UNIVERSAL: can
via UNIVERSAL: isa
  DB<7>
```

Given a class, the m command lists the methods that can be called
against the given class name, with the benefit of not having to
create the object first. In the following example, load FileHandle
and then call m on it:

```
DB<7> use FileHandle
DB<8> m FileHandle
DESTROY
_IOFBF
_IOLBF
_IONBF
_open_mode_string
autoflush
clearerr
close
<...truncated output...>
  DB<9>
```

M

M

Lists all loaded modules, that is, the contents of %INC keyed by the
module name, with the version and actual filename being used in
the value:

```
perldb@monkey> perl -d -e 0
<...truncated output...>
  DB<1> M
'Carp.pm' => '1.01 from /usr/lib/perl5/5.8.0/Carp.pm'
'Carp/Heavy.pm' => '/usr/lib/perl5/5.8.0/Carp/Heavy.pm'
'Exporter.pm' => '5.566 from /usr/lib/perl5/5.8.0/Exporter.pm'
'Term/Cap.pm' => '1.07 from /usr/lib/perl5/5.8.0/Term/Cap.pm'
'Term/ReadLine.pm' => '1.00 from /usr/lib/perl5/5.8.0/Te...
'perl5db.pl' => '1.19 from /usr/lib/perl5/5.8.0/perl5db.pl'
'strict.pm' => '1.02 from /usr/lib/perl5/5.8.0/strict.pm'
'vars.pm' => '1.01 from /usr/lib/perl5/5.8.0/vars.pm'
'warnings.pm' => '1.00 from /usr/lib/perl5/5.8.0/warnings.pm'
'warnings/register.pm' => '1.00 from /usr/lib/perl5/5.8.0/war...
  DB<10>
```

S [[!] ~*pattern*]

Lists either all subroutines that can be called at the current location, or the subroutines that can be constrained by *pattern*.

Typing S with no argument lists all subroutines:

```
perldb@monkey> perl -d -e 0
<...truncated output...>
main::(-e:1):   0
  DB<1> S
AutoLoader::AUTOLOAD
AutoLoader::BEGIN
AutoLoader::__ANON__[/usr/local/lib/perl5/5.8.0/AutoLoader.pm.96]
AutoLoader::import
AutoLoader::unimport
Carp::BEGIN
Carp::caller_info
Carp::carp
Carp::cluck
<...truncated output...>
warnings::__chk
warnings::bits
warnings::enabled
warnings::import
warnings::register::import
warnings::register::mkMask
warnings::unimport
warnings::warn
warnings::warnif
  DB<1>
```

The output of the S command without arguments is likely to be rather long. In this situation, S is normally piped through a pager to control the output (for example, |S). See the later section "Shell and Debugger Commands" for more information on |.

Given a regular expression as an argument, the S command displays subroutines matching the pattern:

```
  DB<1> S ^main
main::BEGIN
main::dumpValue
main::dumpvar
  DB<2> S gs::r
warnings::register::import
warnings::register::mkMask
  DB<3>
```

The pattern can also be negated by prefixing with an exclamation point (!):

```
DB<3> S !gs::r
Carp::BEGIN
Carp::caller_info
Carp::carp
Carp::cluck
Carp::confess
<...truncated output...>
  DB<4>
```

V   Lists variables

V [*pkg* [*vars*]]

Lists all variables in the specified *package*. The current package is the default. my variables are not listed; see also the y command.

Note that all variables are dumped as they would be via the x command:

```
perldb@monkey> perl -d -e 0
<...truncated output...>
  DB<1> V
$/ = '
'
FileHandle(stderr) => fileno(2)
%SIG = (
   'ABRT' => undef
   'ALRM' => undef
   'BUS' => CODE(0x8235cc8)
<...truncated output...>
  DB<2>
```

As the output of V can be verbose when not restricted by *pkg* and *vars*, use of | is recommended.

A package name can be given to restrict the range of variables displayed. The package name, which is case-sensitive, should be given in full:

```
DB<2> V Carp
$MaxArgLen = 64
%Internal = (
   'Exporter' => 1
)
$MaxArgNums = 8
@EXPORT_OK = (
   0 'cluck'
   1 'verbose'
<...truncated output...>
  DB<3>
```

In addition to the package name, a variable name can be given. This is effectively an eq comparison:

```
DB<3> V Carp Verbose
$Verbose = 0
  DB<4>
```

The variable name may also be a regular expression preceded by a ~:

```
DB<4> V Carp ~V
$Verbose = 0
$VERSION = 1.01
  DB<5>
```

X   Dumps expressions

x [*maxdepth*] *expr*

Evaluates the expression in a list context, and dumps it via the standard *dumpvar.pl* library.

Although the output is very similar, it is a common misconception that the debugger uses the Data::Dumper module.

Given an expression as an argument, the x command dumps the given expression. For example, set up a simple scalar variable and dump it:

```
perldb@monkey> perl -d -e 0
<...truncated output...>
main::(-e:1):   0
  DB<1> $bar = '123'
  DR<?> x $bar
0  123
  DB<3>
```

Now define a slightly more complex structure, such as an object with attribute:

```
DB<3> $obj = bless({'foo'=>$bar}, 'FooBar')
DB<4> x $obj
0  FooBar=HASH(0x84ad964)
   'foo' => 123
  DB<5>
```

If you give x a reference, it will dump the expression recursively. See also DumpReused in the later section "Quick Reference":

```
DB<5> x qw(one two three)
0  'one'
1  'two'
2  'three'
  DB<6>
```

In the example below, watch the apparently single-quoted space ' ' naturally resolve into 2 distinct quote characters, which demonstrates how useful it can be to dump the actual variables at runtime, as opposed to simply assuming anything about your incoming data.

```
DB<6> x [qw(one two ' ' three)]
0  ARRAY(0x8333d94)
   0  'one'
   1  'two'
   2  '\''
   3  '\''
   4  'three'
DB<7>
```

Watch how the ARRAY(0x8333d94) hexadecimal numbers (the stringified value of the array reference representing an actual memory address) changes as Perl assigns a fresh memory address to the dynamically created reference:

```
DB<7> x [qw(one two), $bar]
0  ARRAY(0x82d2404)
   0  'one'
   1  'two'
   2  Foo=HASH(0x82d9c88)
      'foo' => 124
DB<8>
```

You can also specify a maximum depth to the x command to restrict how deep the display goes. This is useful when dealing with complicated or nested structures.

Note that the use of 0 (zero) is not useful, as this means the maximum depth is simply ignored.

To illustrate, set up a simple hash reference and dump it:

```
DB<8> $bar = {foo=$foo,depth2=>{depth3=>'here'}})
DB<9> x $bar
0  HASH(0x8331e88)
   'depth2' => HASH(0x832f658)
      'depth3' => 'here'
   'foo' => 124
DB<10>
```

Now restrict the depth to 1 and dump the hash:

```
DB<10> x 1 $bar
0  HASH(0x8331e88)
DB<11>
```

Then dump it with a depth of 2:

```
DB<11> x 2 $bar
0  HASH(0x8331e88)
```

```
    'depth2' => HASH(0x832f658)
    'foo' => 124
  DB<12>
```

Then dump it with a depth of 3:

```
  DB<12> x 3 $bar
0  HASH(0x8331e88)
    'depth2' => HASH(0x832f658)
      'depth3' => 'here'
    'foo' => 124
  DB<13>
```

Dumping a subset of the hash is equally valid. This gives you a great deal of control:

```
  DB<13> x 2 $bar->{depth2}
0  HASH(0x832f658)
    'depth3' => 'here'
  DB<14>
```

As always, if an object or variable is too large to be viewed on a single screen, use the | command to page the output—for example, |x expr. For more information on the | command, see the later section "Shell and Debugger Commands."

X   Dumps the variables in the current package

X [*vars*]

Dumps all variables in the package. This is the same as V *current_ package*:

```
  perldb@monkey> perl -d -e 0
  <...truncated output...>
  DB<1> X
$/ = '
'
FileHandle(stderr) => fileno(2)
%SIG = (
    'ABRT' => undef
    'ALRM' => undef
    'BUS' => CODE(0x8235cc8)
  <...truncated output...>
  DB<2>
```

Given a regular expression (preceded by ~), the X command dumps current package variables filtered by the given pattern:

```
  DB<2> X ~\d
$2 = '~\\d'
$1 = 'main'
$0 = '-e'
  DB<3>
```

---

y [*level* [*vars*]]

Wraps the PadWalker module to display lexical and my variables *n* levels from the current subroutine. The default level is 1.

To demonstrate the y command, you should be in a subroutine so the PadWalker has something to look back up to. Use the *linecounter.pl* program (see "About This Book"), and use c to run the first line of the report( ) subroutine. See the later section "Motion" for an explanation of c:

```
perldb@monkey> perl -d linecounter.pl ^.*\s*mat
<...truncated output...>
main::(linecounter.pl:8):          my @args = @ARGV;
  DB<1> c report
main::report(linecounter.pl:61):                    my $FH = shift;
  DB<2>
```

Now use y to display the my variables from the next level up:

```
  DB<2> y
$REGEX = '^.*s*mat'
$help = 0
$verbose = 0
@args = (
   0  'input_file'
)
@files = (
   0  'input_file'
)
  DB<2>
```

With a numeric argument, you can specify to climb the specified number of levels up the call stack and display the lexical variables defined there. The default is 1 level:

```
  DB<2> y 1
$FH = FileHandle=GLOB(0x83ff090)
   -> *Symbol::GEN0
         FileHandle({*Symbol::GEN0}) => fileno(6)
$REGEX = '^.*s*mat'
$file = 'input_file'
$help = 0
$verbose = 0
@args = (
   0  'input_file'
)
@files = (
   0  'input_file'
)
  DB<3>
```

With a regular expression as a second argument, the variables displayed at the given level may be restricted by that pattern:

```
    DB<3> y 1 ~e
$help = 0
$verbose = 0
@files = (
   0  'input_file'
)
    DB<4>
```

Listing Code and Searching

This section describes commands for listing code or searching for a particular block of code. It covers:

- How to list code anywhere in any file loaded in %INC
- How to list code sequentially and to return to where you started without affecting program execution
- How to search forward and backward through the code

Interpreting code listings

The debugger lists and displays code with a number of hints to help the programmer, as follows:

DB<n>

> The sequential number of the debugger command. See "Shell and Debugger Commands" for information on recalling a command from the history.

n

> Each line of code has the line number in the file on the left hand side.

==>

> Indicates the code that is about to be executed, i.e., the current position.[*]

---

[*] Note that Perl 5.8.0 had a bug in which ==> did not always point to the correct line that was about to be executed. This is fixed in 5.8.1 and for the examples in this book.

:

A breakpoint or action may be set against this line.

:a

An action is currently set against this line.

:b

A breakpoint is currently set against this line.

For information on actions and breakpoints and how to list them, see the later section "Actions, Breakpoints, and Watchpoints."

For example:

```
perldb@monkey> perl -d linecounter.pl
<...truncated output...>
main::(linecounter.pl:8):       my @args = @ARGV;
  DB<1> b 11
  DB<2> a 12 $help
  DB<3> l
8==>    my @args = @ARGV;
9
10      # help requested?
11:b    my $help = grep(/^-h(elp)*$/i, @args);
12:a    if ($help) {
13:             logg(help());
14:             exit 0;
15      }
```

Here use the b and a commands to set up a breakpoint and action before you list it with l. Then when you list the code, see that the next line to be executed is line number 8, that a breakpoint is set on line 11, an action on line 12, and that lines 13 and 14 may have a breakpoint or action set against them.

Now that you know what to look for in code listings, here are the listing and searching commands.

---

l   Lists code

l [*min+incr*|*min-max*|*line*|*subname*|*$var*]

Lists code within the currently loaded file in windowSize chunks. Note that you can always get back to the current code position with the . command (described later in this section).

Sometimes the default windowSize view of your code is just not sufficient, and knowing how to modify the view can make the difference between an easy troubleshooting session and a hard one. See the later section "Quick Reference" for more information about windowSize.

Without any arguments, the l command lists code from a current viewing position:

```
perldb@monkey> perl -d linecounter.pl
<...truncated output...>
main::(linecounter.pl:8):       my @args = @ARGV;
  DB<1> l
8==>    my @args = @ARGV;
9
10      # help requested?
11:     my $help = grep(/^-h(elp)*$/i, @args);
12:     if ($help) {
13:             logg(help());
14:             exit 0;
15      }
16
17      # get the pattern to match against.
  DB<1>
```

To continue the listing from the current point, type l again:

```
  DB<1> l
18:     my $REGEX = shift @args || '';
19
20      # get the files for processing.
21:     my @files = grep(!/^-h(elp)*$/i, @args);
22:     unless (@files) {
23:             push(@files, $0);
24:             logg("using default $0 while no files given");
25      }
26
27      # loop through the files
  DB<1>
```

With a single integer as an argument, the l command lists a single line of code at the specified line:

```
  DB<1> l 11
11:     my $help = grep(/^-h(elp)*$/i, @args);
  DB<2>
```

A range may also be specified. For example, to list the range of code from line number 11 through line number 14, type:

```
  DB<3> l 11-14
11:     my $help = grep(/^-h(elp)*$/i, @args);
12:     if ($help) {
```

```
13:              logg(help());
14:              exit 0;
  DB<4>
```

You receive the same result by telling the debugger to list line number 11 and the three lines following it:

```
DB<2> l 11+3
11:      my $help = grep(/^-h(elp)*$/i, @args);
12:      if ($help) {
13:              logg(help());
14:              exit 0;
  DB<3>
```

To view a particular subroutine, you can supply the subroutine's name to the l command. This lists windowSize lines of code of the given subroutine:

```
DB<4> l report
56       sub report {
57:              my $FH = shift;
58:              my $regex = shift;
59:              my %report = ();
60:              my $i_cnt  = 0;
61:              while (<$FH>) {
62:                      $i_cnt++;
63:                      my $i_match = 0;
64:                      my $line = $_;
65:                      if ($line =~ /($regex)/) {
  DB<5>
```

Note that the subroutine may be in any file loaded in %INC:

```
DB<5> l Carp::croak
Switching to file '/usr/lib/perl5/5.8.0/Carp.pm'.
191:    sub croak   { die  shortmess @_ }
  DB<6>
```

The subroutine can also be referenced by $var. To demonstrate, load the following code into the file *subroutineref.pl*:

```
$sub = sub { print "program: $0\n"; };
```

Run the debugger on it, and use l $sub to list the code:

```
perldb@monkey> perl -d subroutineref.pl
<...truncated output...>
main::(linecounter.pl:8):       my @args = @ARGV;
  DB<1> l $sub
Interpreted as: $sub
2       $sub = sub { print "program: $0\n"; };
3
  DB<2>
```

(Note that although this feature works in 5.6.1, it is broken in 5.8.0, but is fixed again in 5.8.1.)

---

v   Views code window

v [*line*]

Views windowSize lines of code at the current viewing location. v maps to the l command, and attempts to put the current line somewhere above the middle of the window:

```
perldb@monkey> perl -d linecounter.pl
<...truncated output...>
  DB<1> c 11
main::(linecounter.pl:11):      my $help = grep(/^-h(elp)*$/i,
@args);
  DB<2> v
8==>    my @args = @ARGV;
9
10      # help requested?
11:     my $help = grep(/^-h(elp)*$/i, @args);
12:     if ($help) {
13:             logg(help());
14:             exit 0;
15      }
16
17      # get the pattern to match against.
  DB<2>
```

Specify a line number as an argument to view windowSize lines of code at the given line number. v *line* maps to the l *line+windowSize* command, placing the line above the middle of the window:

```
  DB<2> v 18
15==>   }
16
17      # get the pattern to match against.
18:     my $REGEX = shift @args || '';
19
20      # get the files for processing.
21:     my @files = grep(!/^-h(elp)*$/i, @args);
22:     unless (@files) {
23:             push(@files, $0);
24:             logg("using default $0 while no files given");
  DB<3>
```

Although the v command is nearly redundant to l, it replaces the old w command (pre 5.8.0), which merely showed a window of code. The l command has far more functionality, but v has been retained for ease of saying, "view the code around here."

.

With any of the code-listing commands above, it can be easy to flounder in the wealth of detail. The . command resets your viewing location to your current position in the code and displays the next line to execute, without increasing command count:

```
  DB<3> .
main::(linecounter.pl:11): my $help = grep(/^-h(elp)*$/i, @args);
  DB<3>
```

—   Lists previous windowSize lines of code

-

Lists previous lines of code, without increasing command count:

```
  DB<3> -
1       # $Id: listing-code.pod,v 1.38 2003/10/13 14:51:02 pe...
2       #
3       # perl debugger demonstration program
4
5:      use strict;
6:      use FileHandle;
7
8:      my @args = @ARGV;
9
10      # help requested?
  DB<3>
```

/   Searches forwards in code

/regex[/]

Searches forwards for the given regular expression. Note that the trailing slash is optional and that standard regex quoting rules apply:

```
perldb@monkey> perl -d linecounter.pl
<...truncated output...>
main::(linecounter.pl:8):       my @args = @ARGV;
  DB<1> /logg
13:             logg(help( ));
  DB<2>
```

A lone forward slash (/) repeats the forward search without incrementing the command counter:

```
  DB<2> /
24:             logg("using default $0 while no files given");
  DB<2>
```

If the search is unsuccessful before hitting the end of the file, it will start again at the top, once.

For more information on regular expressions, see the *perlre* and *perlretut* manpages.

? Searches backwards in code

?regex[?]

Searches backwards for the given regular expression. Note that the trailing question mark is optional and that standard regex quoting rules apply. This search wraps to the end of the file unless a match is found above:

```
perldb@monkey> perl -d linecounter.pl
<...truncated output...>
main::(linecounter.pl:8):        my @args = @ARGV;
  DB<1> ?logg
94:              logg("Error: $error", @_);
  DB<2>
```

A lone question mark (?) repeats the backwards search without incrementing the command counter:

```
  DB<?> ?
88:     sub logg {
  DB<2>
```

---

f Views file given by the *filename* from those currently loaded in %INC

f *filename*

Searches for the given filename against the currently loaded files or libraries in %INC. The filename can be a regular expression.

The f command does not run the file; it simply loads it to be viewed and perhaps searched. You can still return to your current position with the . command:

```
perldb@monkey> perl -d -e 0
<...truncated output...>
  DB<1> f warnings
Choosing /usr/lib/perl5/5.8.0/warnings.pm matching 'warnings':
    1
    2         # !!!!!!!   DO NOT EDIT THIS FILE   !!!!!!!
    3         # This file was created by warnings.pl
    4         # Any changes made here will be lost.
    5         #
    6
    7         package warnings;
```

```
      8
      9:      our $VERSION = '1.00';
     10
              DB<2>
```

Beware that the file selected is not always what you think it will be. For example, if you're looking for Carp.pm, just using Carp finds the wrong file:

```
DB<2> f Carp
Choosing /usr/lib/perl5/5.8.0/Carp/Heavy.pm matching 'Carp': 1 #
Carp::Heavy uses some variables in common with Carp.  2
package Carp;
  DB<3>
```

Trying an uppercase version does not find it either:

```
DB<3> f CARP.pm
No file matching 'CARP.pm' is loaded.
  DB<4>
```

Finally, using Carp.pm produces the right result:

```
DB<4> f Carp.pm
Choosing /usr/lib/perl5/5.8.0/Carp.pm matching 'Carp.pm': 1
package Carp; 2
  DB<5>
```

Using an explicitly case-insensitive regular expression would perhaps have been an improvement earlier on:

```
DB<5> f (?i:CARP\.pm)
Choosing /usr/lib/perl5/5.8.0/Carp.pm matching '(?i:CARP\.pm)':
1       package Carp; 2
  DB<6>
```

If the file is not loaded yet, you receive an error message:

```
DB<6> f Dumper.pm
No file matching 'Dumper' is loaded.
  DB<7>
```

Load with use and try again:

```
DB<8> use Data::Dumper
DB<9> f Dumper.pm
Choosing /usr/local/lib/perl5/5.8.0/i586-linux/Data/Dumper.pm
matching 'Dumper.pm':
1       #
2       # Data/Dumper.pm
3       #
4       # convert perl data structures into perl syntax...
5       # and eval
6       #
7       # Documentation at the __END__
8       #
```

```
    9
   10       package Data::Dumper;
     DB<10>
```

Now use l Dumper to list the Dumper( ) subroutine:

```
     DB<10> l Dumper
   479     sub Dumper {
   480:       return Data::Dumper->Dump([@_]);
   481     }
     DB<11>
```

Motion

This section describes the motion commands controlling the execution of the program. It covers:

- How to stop and start program execution
- How to step into or across function calls
- Displaying stack traces

Note that the most recent n or s command may be repeated with a simple carriage return.

In this section I mostly use *linecounter.pl* for examples.

---

c   Continues program execution

c [*line*|*sub*]

Continues program execution until told otherwise.

The c command continues program execution until one of the following conditions:

- If a line number is given as an argument, execution stops before that line number.
- If a subroutine name is given as an argument, execution stops at the beginning of the subroutine.
- If a breakpoint is set, it stops at that breakpoint. See the section "Actions, Breakpoints, and Watchpoints" for more information on breakpoints.

- If the $DB::single variable is set for a particular line, it stops at that line to single-step through the program. See the later section "Debugger Variables" for more information.

If none of these conditions are met, the program continues executing until the end of the program.

In this example, first use / to find an appropriate line to stop on, set a breakpoint on it with b, and then use c to move to that position:

```
perldb@monkey> perl -d linecounter.pl ^.*\s*mat input_file
<...truncated output...>
main::(linecounter.pl:8):        my @args = @ARGV;
  DB<1> /grep
11:     my $help = grep(/^-h(elp)*$/i, @args);
  DB<2> b 11
  DB<3> c
main::(linecounter.pl:11): my $help = grep(/^-h(elp)*$/i, @args);
  DB<3>
```

Then continue until the given subroutine is called, and stop at the first line:

```
  DB<3> c report
main::report(linecounter.pl:57):              my $FH = shift;
  DB<4>
```

You can also continue until a specified line is reached:

```
  DB<4> c 65
main::report(linecounter.pl:65):                            if
($line =~ /($regex)/) {
  DB<5>
```

---

n   Steps to the next executable statement

n [*expr*]

Steps over the statement to the next executable statement in the current scope and down one line.

If n encounters a subroutine call, it just steps across it (as opposed to s, which steps into it).

A <CR> (carriage return) repeats the n command, but the command number does not increase with <CR>.

As an example, find a convenient line to stop on, and use c to continue to that line:

```
perldb@monkey> perl -d linecounter.pl ^.*\s*mat input_file
<...truncated output...>
main::(linecounter.pl:8):        my @args = @ARGV;
```

```
   DB<1> /report\(
33:                              my %report = %{report($FH,
$REGEX)}; # -> subroutine
   DB<2> c 33
main::(linecounter.pl:33):                              my
%report = %{report($FH, $REGEX)}; # -> subroutine
   DB<3>
```

Now use n to step over the next line (across the function call):

```
   DB<3> n
main::(linecounter.pl:34):                          if (keys %report) {
   DB<4>
```

Note that placing the expression $DB::single=2 in your code has a similar effect to the n command. See the later section "Debugger Variables" for more information.

If an expression is given as an argument matching the names of function calls used in the program, the debugger stops before each statement within those functions. This is a situation in which using <CR> to repeat the previous n command is especially useful, because it saves you from having to retype the expression repeatedly.

For example, place the following code into the file *nexpr*:

```
sub one {
              print "one\n";
}

sub two {
              print "two\n";
}

sub three {
              print "three\n";
}
```

Run the debugger against it:

```
perldb@monkey> perl -d nexpr
<...truncated output...>
Debugged program terminated.  Use q to quit or R to restart,
auto(-1)
   DB<1> o die?
                              die = 'N/A'
   DB<2>
```

Ignore the spurious messages generated because there is no code to execute in our example, and enter an expression to next step through using the n command:

```
    DB<2> n &one; &two; &three;
main::((eval 4)[/usr/lib/perl5/5.8.1/perl5db.pl:618]:3):
3:      &one; &two; &three;;
    DB<<3>>
```

Use a carriage return to repeat the latest n command and go to the next functional statement:

```
    DB<<3>> <CR>
one
main::((eval 4)[/usr/lib/perl5/5.8.1/perl5db.pl:618]:3):
3:      &one; &two; &three;;
    DB<<3>>
```

The debugger displays nested angle brackets to indicate how deep in an expression we are. Use another carriage return to step across the second function call:

```
    DB<<3>> <CR>
two
main::((eval 4)[/usr/lib/perl5/5.8.1/perl5db.pl:618]:3):
3:      &one; &two; &three;;
    DB<<3>>
```

The third carriage return returns us to the familiar single angle brackets, and the disappearance of the eval message informs us we have reached the end of the expression:

```
    DB<<3>> <CR>
three
    DB<3>
```

The expression is evaluated as a whole if it is irretrievably concatenated together:

```
    DB<3> n &one.&two.&three
main::((eval 5)[/usr/lib/perl5/5.8.1/perl5db.pl:618]:3):
3:      &one.&two.&three;
    DB<<4>>
one
two
three
    DB<4>
```

r

Runs through the current subroutine and stops on returning, printing the return value if PrintRet is true. For more info on PrintRet see "Quick Reference."

As an example, first use c to go to the first line of a subroutine:

```
perldb@monkey> perl -d linecounter.pl ^.*\s*mat input_file
<...truncated output...>
main::(linecounter.pl:8):          my @args = @ARGV;
  DB<1> c report
  main::report(linecounter.pl:59):               my $FH = shift;
  DB<2>
```

Then use r to run through and return from it:

```
  DB<2> r
scalar context return from main::report:    empty hash
main::(linecounter.pl:36):             if (keys %report) {
  DB<2>
```

Note that this is not the equivalent of a Perl return statement. Instead, r tells the debugger to allow the subroutine to resume execution and stop again only once it returns to the scope from where it was called.

---

s   · Steps into the given expression

s [*expr*]

Steps into the next executable statement. Placing the expression $DB::single=1 directly in your code has the same effect; see "Debugger Variables."

As with n, a carriage return (<CR>) repeats the command:

```
perldb@monkey> perl -d linecounter.pl ^.*\s*mat input_file
<...truncated output...>
main::(linecounter.pl:8):          my @args = @ARGV;
  DB<1> /report\(                # find a subroutine to go to
35:                               my %report = %{report($FH,
$REGEX)}; # -> subroutine

  DB<2> c 35                     # go there
main::(linecounter.pl:35):                            my
%report = %{report($FH, $REGEX)}; # -> subroutine
  DB<3> s                       # step into it
main::report(linecounter.pl:59):               my $FH = shift;
  DB<3>
```

If an expression is given that includes function calls, these are also stepped through:

```
perldb@monkey> perl -d linecounter.pl ^.*\s*mat input_file
<...truncated output...>
main::(linecounter.pl:8):        my @args = @ARGV;
  DB<1> s FileHandle->new('./input_file')
main::((eval 19)[/usr/local/lib/perl5/5.8.0/perl5db.pl:17]:3):
3:        FileHandle->new('./input_file');
  DB<2>
```

At this point you can just type <CR> (carriage return) to continue stepping through the code:

```
  DB<2> <CR>
IO::File::new(/usr/local/lib/perl5/5.8.0/i586-linux/IO/File.pm:
136):
136:        my $type = shift;
  DB<2> <CR>
IO::File::new(/usr/local/lib/perl5/5.8.0/i586-linux/IO/File.pm:
137):
137:        my $class = ref($type) || $type || "IO::File";
  DB<2>
```

T Prints stack trace

T

Prints (displays) the current stack trace. See frame and maxTraceLen in "Quick Reference" for ways to modify the output of the trace to make it more readable, and AutoTrace and LineInfo in "Quick Reference" for switching and destination control.

For example, first use c report and c logg to get inside an embedded subroutine:

```
perldb@monkey> perl -d linecounter.pl ^.*\s*mat input_file
<...truncated output...>
main::(linecounter.pl:8):        my @args = @ARGV;
  DB<1> c report
main::report(linecounter.pl:61):        my $FH = shift;
  DB<2> c logg
main::logg(linecounter.pl:93):        print STDOUT join("\n",
@_)."\n" if $verbose;
  DB<3>
```

Now use T to produce a stack trace:

```
  DB<3> T
. = main::logg('^I[1] regex(^.*s*mat) matched(0) <- this is the
first line of the input file^J') called from file `linecounter.
pl' line 75
```

```
$ = main::report(ref(FileHandle), '^.*s*mat') called from file
'linecounter.pl' line 37
  DB<4>
```

Note in the traced display how the . and $ symbols at the left-hand side of the line indicate the context of the called function (. for void, $ for scalar).

The lines in the previous example wrapped because the arguments were so long. For more manageable output, use maxTraceLen:

```
DB<5> o maxTraceLen=20
        maxTraceLen = '20'
DB<6> T
. = main::logg('^I[1] regex(^.*... called from file
`linecounter.pl' line 73
$ = main::report(ref(FileHandle),... called from file
`linecounter.pl' line 35
  DB<7>
```

See "Quick Reference" for more about maxTraceLen.

---

t   Toggle tracing

t [*expr*]

Turns tracing on or off. For an example, turn tracing on:

```
perldb@monkey> perl -d linecounter.pl ^.*\s*mat input_file
<...truncated output...>
main::(linecounter.pl:8):        my @args = @ARGV;
  DB<1> t
Trace = on
  DB<2>
```

Now use c 32 to continue execution until line 32:

```
  DB<1> c 32
main::(linecounter.pl:11):       my $help = grep(/^-h(elp)*$/i,
@args);
main::(linecounter.pl:12):       if ($help) {
main::(linecounter.pl:17):       my $verbose = grep(/^-
v(erbose)*$/i, @args);
main::(linecounter.pl:20):       my $REGEX = shift @args || '';
main::(linecounter.pl:23):       my @files = grep(!/^-
(help|verbose)*$/i, @args);
main::(linecounter.pl:24):       unless (@files) {
main::(linecounter.pl:30):       foreach my $file (@files) {
main::(linecounter.pl:31):           if (-f $file && -r _) {
main::(linecounter.pl:32):               my $FH =
FileHandle->new("< $file");
  DB<2>
```

Note that this is a Perl-level stack trace, which means everything is traced that Perl executes, not just the code you're thinking about.

Stopping at line 32 was advisable as you did not want to trace all the functionality embedded in the FileHandle->new( ) method:

```
DB<2> n
IO::File::new(/usr/local/lib/perl5/5.8.0/i586-linux/IO/File.pm:
136):
136:      my $type = shift;
IO::File::new(/usr/lib/perl5/5.8.0/i586-linux/IO/File.pm:137):
137:      my $class = ref($type) || $type || "IO::File";
IO::File::new(/usr/lib/perl5/5.8.0/i586-linux/IO/File.pm:138):
138:      @_ >= 0 && @_ <= 3
139:          or croak "usage: new $class [FILENAME [,MODE
       [,PERMS]]]";
IO::File::new(/usr/lib/perl5/5.8.0/i586-linux/IO/File.pm:140):
140:      my $fh = $class->SUPER::new( );
   <...truncated output...>
O::File::open(/usr/lib/perl5/5.8.0/i586-linux/IO/File.pm:153):
153:      @_ >= 2 && @_ <= 4 or croak 'usage: $fh->
open(FILENAME [,MODE [,PERMS]])';
IO::File::open(/usr/lib/perl5/5.8.0/i586-linux/IO/File.pm:154):
154:      my ($fh, $file) = @_;
IO::File::open(/usr/lib/perl5/5.8.0/i586-linux/IO/File.pm:155):
155:      if (@_ > 2) {
IO::File::open(/usr/lib/perl5/5.8.0/i586-linux/IO/File.pm:166):
166:      open($fh, $file);
IO::File::new(/usr/lib/perl5/5.8.0/i586-linux/IO/File.pm:145):
145:      $fh;
main::(linecounter.pl:33):                if ($FH) {
   DB<2>
```

See DB::trace in "Debugger Variables" and Devel::Trace in "DB and Devel Namespaces." See also AutoTrace in "Quick Reference" to turn tracing on for the sections of the run of a program.

If you don't want to actually walk through a program, you can also trace an expression given on the fly:

```
perldb@monkey> perl -d linecounter.pl ^.*\s*mat input_file
<...truncated output...>
main::(linecounter.pl:8):          my @args = @ARGV;
   DB<1> t help( )
main::((eval 14)[/usr/local/lib/perl5/5.8.0/perl5db.pl:17]:3):
3:        help( );
main::help(linecounter.pl:85):              return qq|Usage: $0
pattern file [file]+ [-help] [-verbose]|."\n".
main::help(linecounter.pl:86):
qq|Example: perl $0 \^\.*\\s*mat|
   DB<2>
```

Actions, Breakpoints, and Watchpoints

This section describes how you can alter what happens at each line of your program as it runs. It covers:

- How to get the program to stop execution under certain conditions
- How to execute some code when a specific line is reached
- How to do something when a variable takes a particular value
- How to easily watch the value of any variable over time

As with everything else you do with the debugger, all this can be done without having to hardcode this behavior into your program. If you want to monitor a program repeatedly across debugging sessions, simply use the *.perldb* file to initialize the debugger appropriately. Or use the R command to restart the debugging session without exiting the debugger, maintaining any breakpoint, watch expressions, and actions that have been established. See "Shell and Debugger Commands," later in this book, for an explanation of the R command and the *.perldb* file.

To list an action, breakpoint, or watch expression, use the L command, described later in this section.

---

a   Sets an action

`a [line] command [condition]`

An action is any valid Perl command to be executed at a particular line of code. If a line is not given, the default behavior sets an action against the line that is about to be executed. You can only have one action per line.

An optional condition can also be specified, in which case the action only executes if the condition is true. The condition can be any valid Perl expression. Without a specified condition, the condition defaults to 1 and the command is run every time the line is passed.

Without any arguments, the a command returns a usage message. Use L a to list all actions.

A simple example is to print the contents of a variable at a certain line without having to type print $variable continuously. Find a suitable line on which to set an action, and use c to continue execution to that position:

```
perldb@monkey> perl -d linecounter.pl ^.*\s*mat input_file
<...truncated output...>
main::(linecounter.pl:8):           my @args = @ARGV;
  DB<1> /my \$line
68:                    my $line = $_;
  DB<2> c 68
main::report(linecounter.pl:68):                my $line = $_;
  DB<3>
```

Now set the action against the line about to be executed (you don't need to specify a line number in this case):

```
  DB<2> a print "line: $_\n"
  DB<3>
```

Print the current data for reference:

```
  DB<3> p $_
this is the first line of the input file
  DB<4>
```

When you continue to this line again, the $_ variable is printed automatically:

```
  DB<3> c 68
main::report(linecounter.pl:68):                my $line = $_;
line: the second line of the matching file
  DB<4>
```

To delete an action, use the A command (described next).

Although this example is very simple, actions are an extremely powerful tool in debugging. Actions allow you to display and modify any variable conditionally or even to introduce dynamic code, all without touching the source code.

A   Deletes some or all actions

A (line|*)

The A command deletes an action for the given line. For example, suppose you set actions for lines 11 and 30:

```
  DB<1> a 11 print "help($help)\n"
  DB<2> a 30 print "files(@files)\n" if @files
  DB<3>
```

Use the L a command to list all actions:

```
DB<3> L a
linecounter.pl:
 11:    my $help = grep(/^-h(elp)*$/i, @args);
   action:  print "help($help)\n"
 30:    foreach my $file (@files) {
   action:  print "files(@files)\n" if @files
 DB<4>
```

Now use the A command to delete the action on line 11. If you list all actions again, you see that only the action on line 30 remains in effect:

```
DB<4> A 11
DB<5> L
linecounter.pl:
 30:    foreach my $file (@files) {
   action:  print "files(@files)\n" if @files
 DB<5>
```

Without any arguments, the A command prints a usage message. Beware, however, that in versions prior to 5.6.1, this command deletes *all* actions! In Perl 5.6.1 and later, all actions are deleted only when an asterisk is given as an argument:

```
DB<5> A *
 Deleting all actions...
DB<6> L
DB<6>
```

---

b   Sets a breakpoint

h [compile *subname*] | [postpone] *subname* [*condition*]] |
[*line* [*condition*]] | [load *filename*]

A breakpoint stops the program right at runtime, allowing the programmer to inspect variables, modify data, and test "what if" situations at her leisure. Use L b to list all breakpoints.

Breakpoints at specific line numbers

The most common usage of the b command is to set a breakpoint at a certain line number if an optional condition is met. For example, find a suitable line for a breakpoint with /, then use c 66 to continue to the chosen line:

```
perldb@monkey> perl -d linecounter.pl ^.*\s*mat input_file
<...truncated output...>
main::(linecounter.pl:8):        my @args = @ARGV;
  DB<1> /my \$line
```

```
    66:                    my $line = $_;
  DB<2> c 66
main::report(linecounter.pl:66):              my $line = $_;
  DB<3>
```

Now set the conditional breakpoint on the line about to be executed (in this case, line 66). No line number needs to be supplied to the b command in this instance. It is also helpful to print out the value of $_ with p at this point, for reference:

```
  DB<3> b $_ =~ /thi/
  DB<4> p $_
this is the first line of the input file
  DB<5>
```

Next, use c to continue to line 66 once more, and check the value of $_ again to confirm that you have skipped a line and stopped at the appropriate condition:

```
  DB<5> c
main::report(linecounter.pl:66):              my $line = $_;
  DB<6> p $_
third line
  DB<7>
```

If no condition is given, the condition defaults to the expression 1, in which case the program stops execution every time it reaches the specified line. In the next example, use l 63-67 to display the code where you would like to set a breakpoint:

```
perldb@monkey> perl -d linecounter.pl ^.*\s*mat input_file
<...truncated output...>
main::(linecounter.pl:8):     my @args = @ARGV;
  DB<1> l 63-67
63:              while (<$FH>) {
64:                  $i_cnt++;
65:                  my $i_match = 0;
66:                  my $line = $_;
67:                  if ($line =~ /($regex)/) {
  DB<2>
```

Then use b 66 to set the breakpoint and immediately follow this with c to continue to that position:

```
  DB<2> b 66
  DB<3> c
main::report(linecounter.pl:66):              my $line = $_;
  DB<3>
```

Because this breakpoint is unconditional, the debugger stops on this line every time it reaches it:

```
  DB<3> c
main::report(linecounter.pl:66):              my $line = $_;
```

```
    DB<3> c
main::report(linecounter.pl:66):                    my $line = $_;
    DB<3>
```

If you try to set a breakpoint on an unbreakable line, the debugger
complains appropriately:

```
    DB<3> b 550
Line 550 not breakable.
    DB<4>
```

Subroutine breakpoints

You can also set a breakpoint at the first line of given subroutine
name, with an optional condition. For example:

```
perldb@monkey> perl -d linecounter.pl ^.*\s*mat input_file
<...truncated output...>
main::(linecounter.pl:8):           my @args = @ARGV;
    DB<1> b report
    DB<2> b logg $_[0] =~ /\w+/
    DB<3>
```

Here, set a breakpoint for the report subroutine and a conditional breakpoint for the logg subroutine. You can list them for
confirmation:

```
    DB<3> L b
linecounter.pl:
 59:            my $FH = shift;
   break if (1)
 91:            print STDOUT join("\n", @_)."\n" if $verbose;
   break if ($_[0] =~ /\w+/)
    DB<3>
```

Now you can continue running the program, and the debugger
will stop each time you find a breakpoint condition that is true:

```
    DB<3> c
main::logg(linecounter.pl:91):          print STDOUT join("\n",
@_)."\n" if $verbose;
    DB<3> c
main::report(linecounter.pl:59):                    my $FH = shift;
    DB<3> c
main::logg(linecounter.pl:91):          print STDOUT join("\n",
@_)."\n" if $verbose;
    DB<3>
```

In addition to stopping when a subroutine is entered, you can also
set a breakpoint to stop as soon as the given subroutine is
compiled. This is useful for stopping the compilation of the
application and inspecting the environment prior to loading
further libraries and modules—for example, when a subroutine is
created on the fly, or if a module is used or a library is required.

To set a breakpoint at subroutine compilation, you usually need to restart the debugger session with the R command because you've already loaded all prerequisites, executed all use statements, and run all BEGIN blocks. See "Shell and Debugger Commands" for more on the R command. For example:

```
perldb@monkey> perl -d linecounter.pl ^.*\s*mat input_file
<...truncated output...>
main::(linecounter.pl:8):        my @args = @ARGV;
  DB<1> b compile IO::File::new
  DB<2> L
Postponed breakpoints in subroutines:
 IO::File::new  compile
  DB<2> R
Warning: some settings and command-line options may be lost!

Loading DB routines from perl5db.pl version 1.19
Editor support available.

Enter h or 'h h' for help, or 'man perldebug' for more help.

IO::File::CODE(0x817eccc)(/usr/local/lib/perl5/5.8.0/i586-linux/
IO/File.pm:108):
108:    our($VERSION, @EXPORT, @EXPORT_OK, @ISA);
  DB<1>
```

Here you have stopped in the middle of FileHandle compilation.

To demonstrate that your program has not been loaded yet, print the functions available in the main namespace:

```
  DB<1> S main
main::BEGIN
  DB<1>
```

Now continue to the next stopping point (the first executable statement in your program), and print out the same function values:

```
  DB<2> c
main::(linecounter.pl:8):        my @args = @ARGV;
  DB<2> S main
main::BEGIN
main::error
main::help
main::logg
main::report
  DB<3>
```

A variation on b compile is b postpone, in which the debugger stops execution at the first line after compiling the subroutine (as opposed to b compile, where the debugger stops before executing the first statement of the subroutine).

As above, restarting the debugger is often necessary:

```
perldb@monkey> perl -d linecounter.pl ^.*\s*mat input_file
<...truncated output...>
main::(linecounter.pl:8):        my @args = @ARGV;
  DB<1> b postpone IO::File::new
  DB<2> R
Warning: some settings and command-line options may be lost!

Loading DB routines from perl5db.pl version 1.19
Editor support available.
Enter h or 'h h' for help, or 'man perldebug' for more help.

main::(linecounter.pl:8):        my @args = @ARGV;
  DB<1>
```

Now the debugger has stopped at the first executable statement in the program, and it is possible to continue to the set breakpoint:

```
  DB<1> c
IO::File::new(/usr/local/lib/perl5/5.8.0/i586-linux/IO/File.pm:
136):
136:        my $type = shift;
  DB<1>
```

Note the difference between postpone and compile above.

Load breakpoints

Set a breakpoint for the next time a file is loaded. This is useful when you can't get at the guts of a module that is being used within the program, but suspect that it holds the key to the problem.

As above, restarting the debugger is generally necessary, as this breakpoint is not effective until the next time the file is loaded:

```
perldb@monkey> perl -d linecounter.pl ^.*\s*mat input_file
<...truncated output...>
main::(linecounter.pl:8):        my @args = @ARGV;
  DB<1> b load FileHandle
Will stop on load of '/usr/local/lib/perl5/5.8.0/FileHandle.pm
FileHandle FileHandle.pm'.
  DB<2> R
Warning: some settings and command-line options may be lost!

Loading DB routines from perl5db.pl version 1.19
Editor support available.

Enter h or 'h h' for help, or 'man perldebug' for more help.

'/usr/local/lib/perl5/5.8.0/FileHandle.pm' loaded...
FileHandle::CODE(0x817e86c)(/usr/local/lib/perl5/5.8.0/
FileHandle.pm:5):
5:      our($VERSION, @ISA, @EXPORT, @EXPORT_OK);
  DB<1>
```

Note that only one breakpoint may be assigned to a particular line at any time. The most recent breakpoint overwrites previous entries. Also, breakpoints can only be set against executable lines. You can put several conditions against one breakpoint that would resolve to a single condition, but in this case, parentheses are recommended.

See also $DB::single in "Debugger Variables" for information on how to hardwire a breakpoint.

B
Deletes some or all breakpoints

B (*line*|*)

The B command deletes the breakpoint on the given line. For example, first create several breakpoints:

```
perldb@monkey> perl -d linecounter.pl ^.*\s*mat input_file
<...truncated output...>
main::(linecounter.pl:8):          my @args = @ARGV;
  DB<1> b 11
  DB<2> b report
  DB<3> b 66 $_ =~ /\w+/
  DB<4>
```

Then list them to confirm they have been created and (in the case of report) to get the line numbers:

```
  DB<4> L
linecounter.pl:
 11:    my $help = grep(/^-h(elp)*$/i, @args);
   break if (1)
 59:              my $FH = shift;
   break if (1)
 66:                    my $line = $_;
   break if ($_ =~ /\w+/)
  DB<4>
```

Delete a breakpoint by line number, and list them again to confirm that the breakpoint is gone:

```
  DB<4> B 66
  DB<5> L
linecounter.pl:
 11:    my $help = grep(/^-h(elp)*$/i, @args);
   break if (1)
 59:              my $FH = shift;
   break if (1)
  DB<4>
```

Note that breakpoints must be deleted by the line number. To delete the breakpoint for the report subroutine, you have to get the line number first (59 in this instance), and supply the line number to the B command.

Without any arguments, the B command prints a usage message.

To delete all breakpoints, supply an asterisk (*) as the argument:

```
    DB<5> L
linecounter.pl:
  11:        my $help = grep(/^-h(elp)*$/i, @args);
    break if (1)
  59:              my $FH = shift;
    break if (1)
    DB<6> B *
Deleting all breakpoints...
    DB<7> L
    DB<8>
```

Note that in versions prior to 5.6.1, the d and D commands are used to delete breakpoints.

---

w   Sets a watch variable

w [*expr*]

A watch expression, or watchpoint, watches a variable on your behalf. Each time the variable changes, the debugger stops execution (unless NonStop is set—see "Quick Reference") and the pre- and post-values are printed out.

Use | w to list all watchpoints.

To set a watchpoint, supply an argument that evaluates to a variable name:

```
    DB<1> w $line
    DB<2>
```

Use c to continue until the value changes:

```
    DB<2> c
Watchpoint 0:    $line changed:
        old value:     undef
        new value:     'this is the first line of the input file'
main::report(linecounter.pl:67):                        if
($line =~ /($regex)/) {
    DB<2>
```

Note that w only accepts scalar variables until version 5.8.1. Since 5.8.1, w accepts array and hash variables too, but be warned that it treats the hash as an array.

What is perhaps not immediately expected (but is clearly desirable) is that when the variable is *undefined*—for example, when the variable goes out of scope—the watchpoint is triggered again:

```
  DB<2> c
Watchpoint 0:    $line changed:
    old value:      'this is the first line of the input file'
    new value:      undef
main::logg(linecounter.pl:91):            print STDOUT join("\n",
@_)."\n" if $verbose;
  DB<2> c
Watchpoint 0:    $line changed:
      old value:      undef
      new value:      'the second line of the matching file'
main::report(linecounter.pl:67):                     if
($line =~ /($regex)/) {
  DB<2>
```

Note also that the variable watched doesn't need to exist at the time the watchpoint is established. The debugger simply stores the information for later use, and triggers the watchpoint when or if the variable is assigned a value.

Without any arguments, the w command prints a usage message. Note that in versions prior to 5.6.1, w behaved as v does now.

The Tie::Watch module implements a similar functionality to watchpoints. See "DB and Devel Namespaces" for more on Tie::Watch.

You have to be a bit careful when watching a variable across packages (and other scopes), as the variable becomes undefined in the new package and is regarded as a new value in this context.

W   Deletes a watch expression

W (*|*expr*)

The W command deletes some or all watch expressions. Note that the prefix (or sigil) $, @, or % is relevant. A simple variable name var is not enough, because Perl needs to know if you want to delete the watchpoint on the scalar $var, the array @var, or the hash %var:

```
  DB<1> w $var
  DB<2> w @var
  DB<3> w %var
```

```
   DB<4> L w
Watch-expressions:
 $var
 @var
 %var
  DB<5> W $var
  DB<6> L w
Watch-expressions:
 @var
 %var
  DB<7>
```

Use an asterisk (*) as the argument to delete all watch expressions:

```
   DB<9> L w
Watch-expressions:
 @var
 %var
  DB<10> W *
Deleting all watch expressions ...
  DB<11> L w
  DB<12>
```

Without any arguments, W prints out a usage message. Note that in versions prior to 5.6.1, W *expr* creates a watchpoint, and a bare W would delete all of them. Now you must specify the expressions to remove, or use an asterisk to delete all watchpoints.

L   Lists actions, breakpoints, and watch variables

L [a|b|w]

The L command lists actions, breakpoints, and watch variables. Given an argument of a, b, or w, the L command returns just the actions, breakpoints, or watchpoints, respectively. Without any arguments, L returns information on all three.

For example, set up one action, one breakpoint, and one watch-point in a debugger session:

```
perldb@monkey> perl -d linecounter.pl ^.*\s*mat input_file
<...truncated output...>
main::(linecounter.pl:8):          my @args = @ARGV;
  DB<1> l
8==>    my @args = @ARGV;
9
10      # help requested?
11:     my $help = grep(/^-h(elp)*$/i, @args);
12:     if ($help) {
13:             logg(help());
14:             exit 0;
```

```
 15      }
 16
 17:     my $verbose = grep(/^-v(erbose)*$/i, @args);
  DB<1> a 11 print "args(@args)\n"
  DB<2> b 12
  DB<3> w $help
  DB<4>
```

An L on its own lists all actions, breakpoints, and watch variables:

```
  DB<4> L
linecounter.pl:
 11:    my $help = grep(/^-h(elp)*$/i, @args);
   action:  print "args(@args)\n"
 12:    if ($help) {
   break if (1)
Watch-expressions:
 $help
  DB<4>
```

The L a command lists all actions. Lines with breakpoints on them are also returned, because the mechanism for tracking them is related and they are internally regarded more or less the same:

```
  DB<4> L a
linecounter.pl:
 11:    my $help = grep(/^-h(elp)*$/i, @args);
   action:  print "args(@args)\n"
 12:    if ($help) {
  DB<5>
```

The L b command lists all breakpoints. Note that lines with actions on them are also returned, because the mechanism for tracking them is related and they are internally regarded more or less as breakpoints also:

```
  DB<5> L b
linecounter.pl:
 11:    my $help = grep(/^-h(elp)*$/i, @args);
 12:    if ($help) {
   break if (1)
  DB<6>
```

The L w command lists all watch expressions:

```
  DB<6> L w
Watch-expressions:
 $help
  DB<7>
```

Perl, Pre-Prompt, and Post-Prompt Commands

This section describes how to set a command to run before and after each debugger prompt. It covers:

- How to run a Perl command from the debugger prompt
- How to set a Perl command to be executed before and after each prompt
- How to set a debugger command to be executed before each prompt

For both Perl and debugger commands, a multiline command may be entered if \ is entered at the end of the command, in a similar manner to a shell script. (At the time of writing, this feature is broken.)

Running Perl commands

If you wish to access the Perl interpreter at any time during a debugging session, just enter the code directly on the debugger command line. Any command not recognized as a debugger command is assumed to be a Perl command and is passed on to be eval'd by the Perl interpreter. For example:

```
DB<2> print "os: $^O\n"
os: linux
DB<3>
```

If the debugger might interpret your command as a debugger command, you can make sure it sends the command to Perl by preceding the command with a semicolon (;) or a plus sign (+), or by wrapping it in braces such as ( ).

As an example, suppose you created a subroutine called x:

```
DB<3> sub x { print @_, "\n" }
DB<4>
```

If you try to execute the x subroutine directly on the debugger command line, it is interpreted as a debugger command:

```
DB<4> x $^O
0  'linux'
DB<4>
```

To ensure that it is interpreted as a Perl command, prefix it with ; or +:

```
DB<5> ; x $^O
linux
  DB<6>
```

You can also tell the debugger to perform a specific Perl command repeatedly, before or after each debugger prompt. See the "Perl, Pre-Prompt, and Post-Prompt Commands" section.

<   Sets a Perl command to execute before each debugger prompt

< [*expr*|?]

The < command allows you to specify a Perl command to be executed before each debugger prompt. For example:

```
perldb@monkey> perl -d linecounter.pl ^.*\s*mat input_file
<...truncated output...>
main::(linecounter.pl:8):        my @args = @ARGV;
  DB<1> < print "help($help)\n"
  DB<2> n
main::(linecounter.pl:11):       my $help = grep(/^-h(elp)*$/i,
@args);
help()
  DB<2> n
main::(linecounter.pl:12):       if ($help) {
help(0)
  DB<2>
```

If you want to specify additional pre-prompt Perl commands, use the << command, described later in this section.

To display all Perl pre-prompt commands currently set, supply a question mark (?) as the argument:

```
  DB<2> < ?
Perl commands run before each prompt:
        < -- print "help($help)\n"
  DB<3>
```

Beware that in versions of Perl before 5.8.1, if you call the < command without any arguments, all pre-prompt Perl commands are deleted. With Perl 5.8.1 and later, use an asterisk (*) as the argument to delete all commands:

```
  DB<3> < *
All < actions cleared.
  DB<4> < ?
No pre-prompt Perl actions.
  DB<5>
```

<< *expr*

The << command appends Perl commands to the list of commands to execute before each debugger prompt. Note that this command is a bit on the dumb side and just appends the string, even if it is blank. Display the list with < ? and delete all items with < or < *, depending on your version of Perl. For example:

```
    DB<5> < print "help: $help\n"
    DB<6> <?
Perl commands run before each prompt:
        < -- print "help: $help\n"
    DB<7> << print "args: @args\n"
    DB<8> <?
Perl commands run before each prompt:
        < -- print "help: $help\n"
        < -- print "args: @args\n"
    DB<9> <<<>
    DB<10 <?
Perl commands run before each prompt:
        < -- print "help: $help\n"
        < -- print "args: @args\n"
        < --
    DB<11>
```

{ Sets a debugger command to execute before each debugger prompt

{ [*expr*|?]

The { command sets the specified debugger command to be executed before each debugger prompt. For example:

```
perldb@monkey> perl -d linecounter.pl ^.*\s*mat input_file
<...truncated output...>
main::(linecounter.pl:8):        my @args = @ARGV;
  DB<1> { x \@args
  DB<2> n
main::(linecounter.pl:11):       my $help = grep(/^-h(elp)*$/i,
@args);
auto(-1)  DB<2> x \@args
0  ARRAY(0x81c6e6c)
   0  '^.*\s*mat'
   1  'input_file'
  DB<3>
```

If you want to specify additional pre-prompt debugger commands, use the {{ command, described later in this section.

When given a question mark (?) as an argument, the { command displays all debugger pre-prompt commands currently set.

```
    DB<3> { ?
Debugger commands run before each prompt:
        { -- x \@args
    DB<4>
```

Beware that in versions of Perl before 5.8.1, if you call the { command without any arguments, all pre-prompt debugger commands are deleted. With Perl 5.8.1 and later, use an asterisk (*) as the argument to delete all commands.

```
    DB<4> { *
All { actions cleared.
    DB<4> { ?
No pre-prompt debugger actions.
    DB<5>
```

{{   Appends to the list of pre-prompt debugger commands

{{ *expr*

The {{ command allows you to append debugger commands to the list of commands that are executed before each debugger prompt. Display the list with { ?, and delete all items with { or { *, depending on your version of Perl. For example:

```
    DB<5> { x \@args
    DB<6> {?
Debugger commands run before each prompt:
        { -- x \@args
    DB<7> {{ 1
    DB<8> {?
Debugger commands run before each prompt:
        { -- x \@args
        { -- 1
    DB<9> {{
    DB<10> {?
Debugger commands run before each prompt:
        { -- x \@args
        { -- 1
        { --
    DB<11>
```

Note that similar to <<, {{ accepts even a blank line as a command.

> [*expr*|?]

The > command sets a Perl command to execute after each debugger prompt. The behavior of > closely mirrors that of the < command described previously in this section. For example:

```
perldb@monkey> perl -d linecounter.pl ^.*\s*mat input_file
<...truncated output...>
main::(linecounter.pl:8):        my @args = @ARGV;
  DB<1> /if \(\$line            # find the regex line
67:               if ($line =~ /($regex)/) {
  DB<2> > print "matches: 1($1) 2($2) 3($3) 4($4) 5($5)\n"
  DB<3> c 67                    # go to the line
matches: 1() 2() 3() 4() 5()
main::report(linecounter.pl:67):                          if
($line =~ /($regex)/) {
  DB<4> n
matches: 1() 2() 3() 4() 5()
main::report(linecounter.pl:71):
$i_match = 0;
  DB<4>
```

To append additional post-prompt Perl commands, use the >> command, described next. Display all Perl post-prompt commands currently set with > ?:

```
  DB<4> > ?
Perl commands run after each prompt:
    > -- print "matches: 1($1) 2($2) 3($3) 4($4) 5($5)\n"
  DB<5>
```

Beware that in versions of Perl before 5.8.1, if you call the > command without any arguments, all post-prompt Perl commands are deleted. With Perl 5.8.1 and later, use an asterisk (*) as the argument to delete all commands:

```
  DB<5> > *
All > actions cleared.
  DB<5> > ?
No post-prompt Perl actions.
  DB<6>
```

Note there is no command for setting post-prompt debugger commands, as this is deemed redundant.

>> *expr*

The >> command allows you to append to the list of post-prompt Perl commands. Again, the behavior is similar to << and {{, shown previously:

```
    DB<6> > print "argv: @ARGV\n"
    DB<7> >> 1
    DB<8> >>
    DB<9> >?
Perl commands run after each prompt:
       > -- print "argv: @ARGV\n"
       > -- 1
       > --
    DB<10>
```

Shell and Debugger Commands

This section explains how to control the execution of various types of commands from within the debugger. It covers:

- How to execute shell commands from the debugger
- How to use a pager to manage large volumes of data
- How to store commands in a file and run them at startup or during runtime
- How to view the command history, and reuse an old command or alias one command to another
- How to restart the debugger and to retain all current session information

See "Perl, Pre-Prompt, and Post-Prompt Commands" for information on running Perl commands from the debugger.

The .perldb initialization file

At startup, the debugger looks for *.perldb* or *.perldb.ini*. This file may reside either in the current directory or (on Unix machines) in the user's home directory. For security reasons, this file must be owned by *root* or the current user, and can only be writable by the owner.

The DB::parse_options() subroutine may be called from the *.perldb* or *.perldb.ini* file, with a string consisting of any valid PERLDB_OPTS option. See "Setting Options" for information on the o command, "Debugger Variables" for more on PERLDB_OPTS, and "Quick Reference" for more information on available options.

The DB::afterinit() subroutine can be defined in *.perldb*, and it is called after debugger initialization.

Suppose the following code is in the *.perldb* file in the current directory:

```
&parse_options("AutoTrace=0");

sub afterinit {
  print "Welcome to the Perl debugger - may 'the force' be
with you...\n\n";
  push(@DB::typeahead, ('b report', 'w $line', 'H', 'l
report'));
  $trace=0;
}
```

This demonstrates that you can enter options and commands in a couple of different ways.

Note that the DB::typeahead tactic shown here is unsupported although it works very well. A better alternative might be to use the source command, but it probably depends on what you are doing.

When the debugger runs now, it prints a warm welcome message, and then sets a breakpoint on the report() subroutine and a watch expression on the $line variable. Next it lists these commands for history reference, and displays the first 10 lines of the relevant chunk of code:

```
perldb@monkey:~/code> perl -d linecounter.pl ^.*\s*mat input_
file

Loading DB routines from perl5db.pl version 1.19
Editor support available.

Enter h or 'h h' for help, or 'man perldebug' for more help.

Welcome to the Perl debugger - may 'the force' be with you...
```

```
main::(linecounter.pl:10):          my @args = @ARGV;
auto(-4)  DB<1> b report
auto(-3)  DB<2> w $line
auto(-2)  DB<3> H
2: w $line
1: b report
auto(-1)  DB<3> l report
60:     sub report {
61:b            my $FH = shift;
62:             my $regex = shift;
63:             my %report = ();
64:             my $i_cnt   = 0;
65:             while (<$FH>) {
66:                     $i_cnt++;
67:                     my $i_match = 0;
68:                     my $line = $_;
69:                     if ($line =~ /($regex)/) {
  DB<4>
```

Now a single c command brings you to the first line of the
report( ) subroutine, and the next c takes you directly to the
place where the $line variable is first changed:

```
  DB<4> c
main::report(linecounter.pl:61):          my $FH = shift;
  DB<4> c
Watchpoint 0:     $line changed:
    old value:       undef
    new value:       'this is the first line of the input file'
main::report(linecounter.pl:69):                    if
($line =~ /($regex)/) {
  DB<4>
```

Note how you are able to display variables and control the
flow of the program without touching it. It is now possible to
change the contents of the incoming line, perhaps to test a
what if scenario:

```
  DB<4> $line = "this is now the changed line"
  DB<5> n
  Watchpoint 0:    $line changed:
    old value:       'this is the first line of the input file'
    new value:       'this is now the changed line'
  main::report(linecounter.pl:73):
$i_match = 0;
  DB<5>
```

|dbcmd [*args*]

When output from a command is expected to be quite extensive/verbose, you can pipe it through an external pager program. Common pagers on Unix are the *more* and *less* commands, but you can set it to anything you want (see "Quick Reference").

Pagers allow you to page through the output of commands that print a large number of lines without seeing all the information fly off the top of the screen. For example, it is useful when x is used on a deeply nested data structure or a large array, or for viewing the extensive help documentation with h. The output of the debugger command is piped to the pager, allowing you to view it more easily:

```
perldb@monkey> perl -d -e 0
<...truncated output...>
  DB<1> | h h
Help is currently only available for the new 580 CommandSet,
if you really want old behaviour, presumably you know what
you're doing ?-)
T               Stack trace.
s [expr]        Single step [in expr].
<...truncated output...>
                Evals (with saved bodies) are considered to be
filenames:
lines 1-26
<...truncated output...>
  DB<2>
```

Note that you may need to quit the pager explicitly (e.g., with the pager's q command) to return to the debugger prompt.

||dbcmd [*args*]

The || command is similar to |, but DB::OUT is selected as well. For example:

```
  DB<2> ||V
$/ = '
'
FileHandle(stderr) => fileno(2)
%SIG = (
   'ABRT' => undef
   'ALRM' => undef
   'BUS' => CODE(0x8235cc4)
```

```
      -> &DB::diesignal in 0
<...truncated output...>
Can't close DB::OUT
Pager `|less' failed: shell returned -1  # <- ignore the error
message
  DB<3>
```

!!   Runs an external or shell command in a subprocess

!! *cmd*

The !! command runs an external command in a subprocess. Be careful not to confuse this with the ! command.

The !! command reads from $DB::IN and writes to $DB::OUT:

```
perldb@monkey> perl -d -e 0
<...truncated output...>
  DB<1> !!pwd
/home/perldb
  DB<2>
```

See also *shellBang* and *recallCommand* in "Quick Reference."

---

source   Sources debugger commands from another file

source *file*

The source command reads debugger commands from a file and executes them. This is very useful when you have a series of commands you want to run repeatedly. You can type them into a file and then source the file whenever you wish to execute them.

Commands run via source go into your debugger command history, and the command line numbers increment. Sourced files may be nested. No semicolon is needed at the end of lines.

For example, suppose you store the following in a file called *.dbgrc*:

```
w $line
source .breakpoints
L
```

Then store the following in a file called *.breakpoints*:

```
b 67 $line =~ /\w+/
b report
```

Now source the *.dbgrc* file from within the debugger session. (*.dbgrc* sources the *.breakpoints* file, so we don't need to explicitly source it as well.)

```
perldb@monkey> perl -d linecounter.pl ^.*\s*mat input_file
<...truncated output...>
main::(linecounter.pl:8):            my @args = @ARGV;
  DB<1> source .dbgrc
>> w $line
>> source .breakpoints
>> b 67 $line =~ /\w+/
>> b report
>> L
linecounter.pl:
 59:            my $FH = shift;
   break if (1)
 67:                    if ($line =~ /($regex)/) {
   break if ($line =~ /\w+/)
Watch-expressions:
 $line
  DB<7>
```

Once the *.dbgrc* file is sourced, several watch expressions and breakpoints are set up, which is confirmed by the L listing. Continue to the first breakpoint with the c command as usual:

```
  DB<7> c
main::report(linecounter.pl:59):            my $FH = shift;
```

A second c continues execution until the watch expression stops the debugger as the value changes:

```
  DB<7> c
Watchpoint 0:    $line changed:
      old value:     undef
      new value:     'this is the first line of the input file'
main::report(linecounter.pl:67):                    if
($line =~ /($regex)/) {
  DB<7>
```

H   History of commands, recall, and aliases

H [-*number*]

The H command displays the history of commands previously executed in this debugging session. History records are only kept for commands longer than one character. n, l, and x commands are not kept in history.

To actually reuse a command from the history, see the ! command.

For example, use the previous example (from source):

```
perldb@monkey> perl -d linecounter.pl ^.*\s*mat input_file
<...truncated output...>
main::(linecounter.pl:8):            my @args = @ARGV;
```

```
    DB<1> source .dbgrc
>> w $line
>> source .breakpoints
>> b 67 $line =~ /\w+/
>> b report
>> L
linecounter.pl:
 59:              my $FH = shift;
   break if (1)
 67:                      if ($line =~ /($regex)/) {
   break if ($line =~ /\w+/)
Watch-expressions:
 $line
  DB<7>
```

You can display your history with the H command:

```
    DB<7> H
5: b report
4: b 67 $line =~ /\w+/
3: source .breakpoints
2: w $line
1: source .dbgrc
  DB<7>
```

The H command takes an argument of a negative integer, in which case it displays only the given number of commands. The highest number is the most recent command, including this one. For example:

```
    DB<7> H -3
7: H -3
5: b report
4: b 67 $line =~ /\w+/
```

!   Recalls a previous command from the history list

! [[-]number | pattern]

The ! command repeats a command from the history list. The command to be repeated can be specified either with its number in the history or with a pattern. With no arguments, the most recent command is repeated.

As a demonstration, start by setting up a couple of commands:

```
perldb@monkey> perl -d linecounter.pl ^.*\s*mat input_file
<...truncated output...>
main::(linecounter.pl:8):        my @args = @ARGV;
  DB<1> l 8+4
8==>    my @args = @ARGV;
9
10      # help requested?
```

```
11:    my $help = grep(/^-h(elp)*$/i, @args);
12:    if ($help) {
  DB<2> x \@args
0  ARRAY(0x83551d8)
      empty array
  DB<3> n
main::(linecounter.pl:11):       my $help = grep(/^-h(elp)*$/i,
@args);
  DB<3>
```

Now display the history listing for reference, noting how single character commands are ignored:

```
  DB<3> H
2: x \@args
1: l 8+4
  DB<3>
```

The ! command with no arguments repeats the most recent command:

```
  DB<3> !
x \@args
0  ARRAY(0x81c6e64)
   0  '^.*s*mat'
   1  'input_file'
  DB<4>
```

With an argument of a negative integer, the ! command repeats the number-to-last command. For example, ! -7 at a DB<8> prompt repeats command number 2:

```
  DB<4> ! -1
l 8+4
8:    my @args = @ARGV;
9
10    # help requested?
11:    my $help = grep(/^-h(elp)*$/i, @args);
12:    if ($help) {
  DB<5>
```

With a pattern as an argument, the ! command repeats the last command that started with the given pattern. Note that the pattern starts immediately after the exclamation mark, including spaces!

```
  DB<5> !x
x \@args
0  ARRAY(0x81c6e64)
   0  '^.*s*mat'
   1  'input_file'
  DB<6>
```

Do not confuse ! with the !! command, which executes shell commands.

See also recallCommand in "Quick Reference."

Setting Options

There are many options available in the debugger that can modify the debugger's behavior. The options are listed fully in the section "Debugging Options." Within a debugger session, options can be set using the o command. They can also be set on the debugger command line and in *.perldb* initialization files.

---

o   Sets an option

o [*opt*|*opt?*|*opt=val*|*opt="val"*]

The o command sets a debugger option. The syntax to assign an option differs depending whether it is being set to a Boolean or string value.

Option keys are case-insensitive and may be shortened to a unique value.

For example, to assign an option to a string:

```
perldb@monkey> perl -d -e 0
<...truncated output...>
  DB<1> o LineInfo="./db.out"
        LineInfo = './db.out'
  DB<2>
```

When the value includes whitespace, it must be quoted, and any use of similar quotes within the string must be escaped.

To set a Boolean option:

```
DB<2> o AutoTrace
      AutoTrace = '1'
DB<3>
```

You can also use the syntax *opt*=1. The *opt*=1 syntax is preferable to avoid confusion.

To display the current value of an option:

```
DB<3> o pager?
        pager = '|less'
DB<4>
```

Do no include a space when querying Boolean values. The debugger interprets it to mean that you intend to set the option:

```
DB<4> o auto?
        AutoTrace = '0'
DB<5> o auto ?
        AutoTrace = '1'
   Invalid option '?'
DB<6>
```

Although the debugger correctly complains about the invalid option, it has already set the Boolean variable.

Note that you can set more than one option at a time:

```
DB<6> o pager=more autotrace=0
            pager = '|more'
        AutoTrace = '0'
DB<7>
```

With no arguments, the debugger displays the current value of all options:

```
DB<7> o
        hashDepth = 'N/A'
        arrayDepth = 'N/A'
        CommandSet = '580'
    <...truncated output...>
        RemotePort = 'N/A'
        windowSize = '10'
DB<8>
```

Debugger Variables

There are several environment variables and internal debugger variables that control debugger behavior. This section covers:

- Which DB::* variables are available in the public interface
- How to write and run your own debugger library
- What options are available only at startup time
- How to get memory usage information from your Perl program

Note that most debugger interface variables reside in the DB::
namespace, as opposed to being lexically scoped, to give the
programmer the ability to access them from the outside
world. This means the program can invoke debugger functions itself (when it is running under the debugger of course).

Many internal debugger variables are not covered in this
book, because they are not relevant to actually using the
debugger. For example, the debugger uses a special data
structure to hold breakpoints and actions: @{$main::{'_<'.
$file}}. However, there is no reason for a user to access it.
If you are really curious, see the various debugger documentation sources listed in "References" for an explanation of
these structures and other internal mechanisms.

$DB::* Variables

DB::* variables are public interface variables for use with the
debugger. They may be set directly in the code or can be
assigned manually, in an interactive session. They are also
often set as a side-effect from using particular debugger
commands.

Note that if the Perl debugger has not been invoked, the DB::*
variables are completely ignored and declaring or altering
them does absolutely nothing. Therefore, they are perfectly
safe to leave in production code.

$DB::single   Tells debugger to single-step through the next line

`$DB::Single=[1 | 2]`

The debugger stops when it comes to a line where $DB::single is
set to 1 or 2. The default value of $DB::single is 0, in which case
the debugger does not stop.

When $DB::single is set to 1, the debugger stops and behaves as if
you had just typed the s command and wish to single-step
through the next executable line. See "Motion" for an explanation of the s command.

Suppose you had inserted $DB::single=1 at line 35 in the program *linecounter.pl*, just before the call to the report( ) function:

```
35:    $DB::single=1;
36:    my %report = %{report($FH, $REGEX)}; # -> subroutine
37:    if (keys %report) {
```

Now, every time we run this under the debugger, we could run straight to this breakpoint with a single c command.

```
perldb@monkey> perl -d linecounter.pl ^.*\s*mat input_file
<...truncated output...>
main::(linecounter.pl:8):         my @args = @ARGV;
  DB<1> c
main::(linecounter.pl:36):                        my
%report = %{report($FH, $REGEX)}; # -> subroutine
  DB<1>
```

This is very useful when the approximate location of an problem is known, or when you expect to have to return to a particular point in the program while testing or debugging. Just set $DB::single=1 at this point and the debugger will stop there each time the program is run. Like all $DB::* variables, the $DB::single variable is completely ignored when the program is not running under the debugger, so it is safe to hardcode into the program during development and testing, and even in production.

When $DB::single is set to 2, the debugger stops as if you had just typed the n command, and awaits further instructions. $DB::single is also set to 2 as a by-product of typing n. See "Motion" for more on the n command.

In this example, place $DB::single=2 to take effect on each line of each input file in *linecounter.pl* at line 67 only if it contains the string "matching" on the line:

```
66:    my $line = $_;
67:    $DB::single=2 if $line =~ /matching/;
68:    if ($line =~ /($regex)/) {
```

When you run the program in the debugger now, you can run straight there:

```
perldb@monkey> perl -d linecounter.pl ^.*\s*mat input_file
<...truncated output...>
main::(linecounter.pl:8):         my @args = @ARGV;
  DB<1> c
main::report(linecounter.pl:68):                        if
($line =~ /($regex)/) {
  DB<1> p $line1
the second line of the matching file
  DB<2>
```

$DB::signal

`$DB::signal=1`

$DB::signal is a bit like assigning $DB::single=2. Setting either $DB::single or $DB::signal directly in the code stops the debugger, even when it is in the middle of a NonStop run (see "Quick Reference"). The $DB::signal variable is rarely used explicitly; instead, it is usually set via a signal handler on your behalf.

$DB::trace

`$DB::trace=[0 | 1]`

$DB::trace is a Boolean variable that controls whether tracing is turned on. Its default value is 0, in which case tracing is off. It is automatically set to 1 when the AutoTrace option is set and the t command is used. See "Quick Reference" for more on AutoTrace and "Motion" for more on the t command.

For example, suppose you turn on the AutoTrace option with the o command (see "Quick Reference"):

```
perldb@monkey> perl -d linecounter.pl ^.*\s*mat input_file
<...truncated output...>
main::(linecounter.pl:8):        my @args = @ARGV;
  DB<1>  o AutoTrace
            AutoTrace = '1'
  DB<2>
```

The debugger now prints out a stack trace for each line it executes:

```
  DB<2>  p $DB::trace
main::((eval 26)[/usr/local/lib/perl5/5.8.0/perl5db.pl:17]:2):
2:      print {$DB::OUT}  $DB::trace;
1
  DB<3>
```

The $DB::trace variable can be set directly in the program. Setting this variable directly in the code controls the amount of information you receive when you turn tracing on for just on chunk of code. In this example, wrap the report() function call from *linecounter.pl* in a couple of $DB::trace statements:

```
35:         $DB::trace = 1 if $file =~ /input/;
36:         my %report = %{report($FH, $REGEX)}; # ->
subroutine
37:         $DB::trace = 0;
```

If you use the c command the debugger runs straight through the program and turns tracing on and off appropriately, printing out each executed line.

Note that setting AutoTrace=1 sets $DB::trace=1, but setting $DB::trace=1 has no effect on the value of the AutoTrace option.

Tracing can produce prohibitively verbose information unless used carefully. In this example, the execution of the entire while loop is printed for each line of the file:

```
perldb@monkey> perl -d linecounter.pl ^.*\s*mat input_file
<...truncated output...>
main::(linecounter.pl:8): my @args = @ARGV;
  DB<1> c
main::(linecounter.pl:36):                  my %report =
        %{report($FH, $REGEX)}; # -> subroutine
main::report(linecounter.pl:61):     my $FH = shift;
main::report(linecounter.pl:62):     my $regex = shift;
main::report(linecounter.pl:63):     my %report = ();
main::report(linecounter.pl:64):     my $i_cnt  = 0;
main::report(linecounter.pl:65):     while (<$FH>) {
main::report(linecounter.pl:66):         $i_cnt++;
main::report(linecounter.pl:67):         my $i_match = 0;
main::report(linecounter.pl:68):         my $line = $_;
main::report(linecounter.pl:69):         if ($line =~
        /($regex)/) {
main::report(linecounter.pl:73):             $i_match = 0;
main::report(linecounter.pl:75):             logg("\t[$i_cnt]
        regex($regex) matched($i_match) <- $line");
main::logg(linecounter.pl:93):   print STDOUT join("\n",
        @_)."\n" if $verbose;
main::report(linecounter.pl:65):     while (<$FH>) {
main::report(linecounter.pl:66):         $i_cnt++;
main::report(linecounter.pl:67):         my $i_match = 0;
main::report(linecounter.pl:68):         my $line = $_;
main::report(linecounter.pl:69):         if ($line =~
        /($regex)/) {
main::report(linecounter.pl:70):             $report{$i_cnt} =
        $1; #
main::report(linecounter.pl:71):             $i_match++;
main::report(linecounter.pl:75):             logg("\t[$i_cnt]
        regex($regex) matched($i_match) <- $line");
main::logg(linecounter.pl:93):   print STDOUT join("\n",
        @_)."\n" if $verbose;

  <...truncated output...>

main::report(linecounter.pl:65):     while (<$FH>) {
main::report(linecounter.pl:77):     $FH->close;
IO::Handle::close(/usr/local/lib/perl5/5.8.0/i586-linux/
  IO/Handle.pm:359):
```

```
359:        @_ == 1 or croak 'usage: $io->close()';
IO::Handle::close(/usr/local/lib/perl5/5.8.0/i586-linux/
  IO/Handle.pm:360):
360:        my($io) = @_;
IO::Handle::close(/usr/local/lib/perl5/5.8.0/i586-linux/
  IO/Handle.pm:362):
362:        close($io);
main::report(linecounter.pl:78):        return \%report;
main::(linecounter.pl:37):              $DB::trace = 0;
  2               the second line of the mat
Debugged program terminated.  Use q to quit or R to restart,
 use O inhibit_exit to avoid stopping after program termination,
 h q, h R or h O to get additional info.
  DB<1>
```

To get a similar effect without having to type either the c or the q at the end, you could use NonStop (see "Options"):

```
perldb@monkey> PERLDB_OPTS=NonStop perl -d linecounter.pl ^.*\
s*mat input_file
<...truncated output...>
main::(linecounter.pl:8):        my @args = @ARGV;
<...truncated output...>
perldb@monkey>
```

The debugger would run right through and return to the shell with no intervention necessary.

$DB::fork_TTY   Tells debugger to follow a forked process

$DB::fork_TTY=*path*

The $DB::fork_TTY command tells the debugger to spawn a new *xterm* or *OS/2* console for each forked process it comes across during program execution.

Setting up the debugger to follow a forked process in anything other than an *xterm* or an *OS/2* console is fraught with problems. For that reason, this behavior is only supported on Unix systems running the X Window System and on OS/2 machines.

If you simply start a Perl program that forks with -d, by default it attempts to create a new *xterm* window for each forked process.

You can define which TTY to use by giving the correct path in the $DB::fork_TTY variable. You can also supply the path via the function DB::get_fork_TTY.

Using the following code placed in the file *forker.pl*, supply the TTY via an environment variable to get a feel for how this works:

```
unless ($ENV{fork_TTY} =~ /\w+/) {
  die "Usage: fork_TTY=tty perl -d ./forker.pl"; # /dev/pts/9 }

sub DB::get_fork_TTY { return $ENV{fork_TTY}; }

my $pid;
if ($pid = fork) {
  print "PARENT($$) setoff a child($pid) process\n";
  $DB::single=2;
  my $waited = waitpid($pid,0);
  print "PARENT($$) waited for child($waited)\n";
} else {
  die "cannot fork: $!" unless defined $pid;
  sleep(1);                    #
  print "CHILD ($$) running...\n";
  $DB::single=2;
  print "CHILD ($$) done\n";
}

exit 0;
```

If there is an available console at */dev/pts/6* running, the following command should present you with two debugger sessions, giving you a feel for how this works:

```
perldb@monkey> fork_TTY=/dev/pts/6 perl -d forker.pl
<...truncated output...
  DB<1> c
PARENT(1914) setoff a child(1915) process
main::(forker.pl:16):        my $waited = waitpid($pid,0);
  DB<1> CHILD (1915) running...
1
16==>            my $waited = waitpid($pid,0);
17:              print "PARENT($$) waited for child($waited)\n";
18      } else {
19:          die "cannot fork: $!" unless defined $pid;
20:          sleep(1);                    #
21:          print "CHILD ($$) running...\n";
22:          $DB::single=2;
23:          print "CHILD ($$) done\n";
24      }
25
  DB<1>
```

In the parent process, you can confirm your process ID:

```
DB<1> p "my_parent_id: $$"
  my_parent_id: 1914
DB<2>
```

You can also confirm the child process:

```
  DB<2> p "child_id: $pid"
child_id: 1915
  DB<3>
```

Problems with forked TTYs

If the debugger window cannot be created, or there is some other problem, the debugger displays an error message something like this:

```
perldb@monkey> fork_TTY=unset perl -d forker.pl
<...truncated output...>
main::(forker.pl:6):        my $pid;
  DB<1> c
PARENT(1381) setoff a child(1382) process
main::(code/forker.pl:10):                  my $waited =
waitpid($pid,0);
  DB<1> CHILD (1382) running...
######### Forked, but do not know how to create a new TTY.
#########
  Since two debuggers fight for the same TTY, input is severely
entangled.

  I know how to switch the output to a different window in
xterms and OS/2 consoles only.  For a manual switch, put the
name of the created TTY in $DB::fork_TTY, or define a function
DB::get_fork_TTY() returning this.

  On UNIX-like systems one can get the name of a TTY for the
given window by typing tty, and disconnect the shell from TTY by
sleep 1000000.

main::(code/forker.pl:17):              print "CHILD ($$) done\n";
```

Naturally, this example is insufficient if you need to fork more than a single process, but it should prove a reasonable starting point.

Patches are welcome to make this more user-friendly and portable. If you're interested in helping to improve the functionality of this feature, talk to the people on the Perl 5 Porters mailing list (see "References").

Environment Variables

Several environment variables affect how and which debugger is initially loaded. See your shell's documentation for further details on how to set environment variables. On Unix, a typical invocation under the *bash* shell might be:

```
export VARNAME=VALUE
```

PERL5DB

The PERL5DB environment variable defines code containing the debugger to be run. If this variable is not set, the following code is inserted before the first line of the program to be debugged:

```
BEGIN {require 'perl5db.pl'}
```

This calls in the default Perl debugger supplied with the source distribution, unless it has been modified or replaced. All the standard places are searched to find the appropriate library file. You can see the libraries Perl will look in with this command:

```
perldb@monkey> perl -e 'print join("\n", @INC)'
```

You can tell Perl which debugger to use by setting the PERL5DB variable to point to the correct library. If you have written your own debugger and put it in a file called *./my_perl5db.pl*, you can enable it like this in the *bash* shell:

```
export PERL5DB="BEGIN {require './my_perl5db.pl'}"
```

If the debugger cannot be found, Perl complains:

```
perldb@monkey> PERL5DB='BEGIN { require "./missing_perl5db_
library" }' perl -d -e 0
Can't locate ./missing_perl5db_library in @INC (@INC contains:
/usr/local/lib/perl5/5.8.0/i586-linux /usr/local/lib/perl5/
5.8.0/usr/local/lib/perl5/site_perl/5.8.0/i586-linux/usr/local/
lib/perl5/site_perl/5.8.0 /usr/local/lib/perl5/site_perl .).
BEGIN failed--compilation aborted.
perldb@monkey>
```

The primary hook the debugger provides for Perl is a single subroutine, which is called for each line of the program to be debugged. This subroutine, living in the DB package, has the name DB, and it can be redefined on the fly. Here is the classic example that prints the number of lines of code executed so far (borrowed from the *perldebug* manpage):

```
export PERL5DB='BEGIN { sub DB::DB { print "line ".++$line."\n";
} }'
```

This produces the following (albeit only marginally useful) output:

```
perldb@monkey> perl -d linecounter.pl ^.*\s*mat input_file
  line 1
  line 2
  line 3
  line 4
<...truncated output...>
perldb@monkey>
```

Here is an extended example giving more useful information:

```
export PERL5DB='BEGIN{sub DB::DB {my($p,$f,$l)=caller;print
++$i.": <$l> ".(@{"::_<$f"}->[$l])}}'
```

This runs through the entire execution of the program printing the line count, the line number, and each line of code as it goes. It gives output similar to the following:

```
perldb@monkey> perl -d linecounter.pl ^.*\s*mat input_file
1: <6> use FileHandle;
2: <46>    no strict 'refs';
<...truncated output...>
177: <8> my @args = @ARGV;
178: <11> my $help = grep(/^-h(elp)*$/i, @args);
179: <12> if ($help) {
180: <17> my $verbose = grep(/^-v(erbose)*$/i, @args);
181: <20> my $REGEX = shift @args || '';
182: <23> my @files = grep(!/^-(help|verbose)*$/i, @args);
183: <24> unless (@files) {
184: <30> foreach my $file (@files) {
185: <31>        if (-f $file && -r _) {
186: <32>            my $FH = FileHandle->new("< $file");
187: <136>   my $type = shift;
188: <137>   my $class = ref($type) || $type || "IO::File";
<...truncated output...>
272: <322> sub DESTROY { }
273: <30> foreach my $file (@files) {
274: <82> exit 0;
perldb@monkey>
```

See AutoTrace in "Quick Reference" and Devel::Trace in "DB and Devel Namespaces" for similar functionality with more control.

For more ideas on building your own Perl debugger, and to see what other uses people can find for the built-in hooks Perl provides, see "DB and Devel Namespaces."

PERLDB_OPTS   Specifies options for the debugger

After starting the debugger, Perl looks in the PERLDB_OPTS environment variable for any valid options. If the PERLDB_OPTS variable is defined, the debugger runs the DB::parse_options() function on them. The DB::parse_options() function can also be manually enforced by calling it directly in the *.perldb* file.

Note that the PERLDB_OPTS variable is parsed after the *.perldb* file is read. That is, an option set in the *.perldb* file is overridden by an entry in this environment variable. For the complete sequence of events, see "DB and Devel Namespaces."

The classic example is to run your program without intervention (NonStop=1), with trace output (AutoTrace), and entry into each subroutine (f=2) into *db.out* via *LineInfo*. For more information on these see "Quick Reference."

Note that the options may be used by their shortest unique name, although this is not recommended:

```
perldb@monkey> export PERLDB_OPTS='Non Auto f=2 Line=db.out'
perldb@monkey> perl -d linecounter.pl ^.*\s*mat input_file
    2       the second line of the mat
perldb@monkey>
```

Now everything is in the file *db.out*, and you can view this information with any standard editing program or utility available on the system. Use *wc* to count the 2727 lines in the file, and view the first 10 lines with *head*:

```
perldb@monkey> wc db.out
    2727   13390  123156 db.out
perldb@monkey> head db.out
entering CODE(0x817e7d8)
  5:      use strict;
Package /usr/local/lib/perl5/5.8.0/strict.pm.
  93:     $strict::VERSION = "1.02";
  95:     my %bitmask = (
  96:     refs => 0x00000002,
  97:     subs => 0x00000200,
  98:     vars => 0x00000400,
  99:     );
  117:    1;
perldb@monkey>
```

For other possibilities, see the "Quick Reference" section.

PERL_DEBUG_MSTATS   Reports memory information

If the PERL_DEBUG_MSTATS environment variable is set to a value greater than 1 (before and after the program execution), the debugger supplies information on how much memory your program is using.

This only works if your Perl installation has been compiled with Perl's malloc function. You can compile Perl to use its own malloc by passing -Dusemymalloc or -DMYMALLOC at compile time.

See the *INSTALL* file in the Perl distribution for more information on compiling Perl:

```
perldb@monkey> PERL_DEBUG_MSTATS=2  /opt/perl591malloc/bin/
perl5.9.0 linecounter.pl ^.*\s*mat input_file
Memory allocation statistics after compilation: (buckets 4(4)..
8188(8192)
  19072 free:     36    59    63    15     7   3   4     2   2 0 0
                 478    66    15    17    15
 769756 used:    984  1084  5922  1814    89  53  40   220   2 0 3
                 544   614  3470   949    35
Total sbrk(): 804864/80:127. Odd ends: pad+heads+chain+tail:
0+9892+0+6144.
       2          the second line of the mat
Memory allocation statistics after execution:   (buckets 4(4)..
8188(8192)
  14588 free:     31    53    58    12     4   2   3     2   1 0 0
                 472    57     9     9    13
 774240 used:    989  1090  5927  1817    92  54  41   220   3 0 3
                 550   623  3476   957    37
Total sbrk(): 804864/80:127. Odd ends: pad+heads+chain+tail:
0+9892+0+6144.
perldb@monkey>
```

For an explanation of this, see the *perldebguts* manpage.

Here are several suggestions for gaining more information about the memory usage of your Perl program:

UsageOnly

> Obtain memory information on currently loaded package. See UsageOnly in "Quick Reference."

-DL

> Displays "alternative" memory usage. To use this feature, Perl must have been compiled with the -DDEBUGGING flag. You also must code in warn('!') statements for this to be effective. See the *perldebguts* and *perlrun* manpages.

Devel::Peek

> Although the mstats() function (which produces similar output to that above) requires Perl to be compiled with DEBUGGING_MSTATS, the other functions provided by Devel:: Peek enable variables to be dumped as raw datatypes.

Debugging Options

This section describes the options that the debugger uses to define its behavior. Knowing what options are available and how they can be modified increases the efficiency of any debugging session. This section covers:

- Startup options
- The options affecting the printing of dumped data structures
- Controlling the behavior of the debugger when execution is interrupted
- Having the debugger run automatically without user input
- Defining how much trace and prompt information is written and where it's sent

To set options in the debugger, use the o command or the *.perldb* initialization file. See "Setting Options" and "Shell and Debugger Commands" for more information.

Some options can only be set at startup. That is, they must be assigned through the PERLDB_OPTS environment variable (see "Debugger Variables") and the *.perldb* file (see "Shell and Debugger Commands"). The options that can only be set at startup are NonStop, noTTY, ReadLine, RemotePort, and TTY.

---

arrayDepth   Defines depth in dumping arrays

The arrayDepth option defines how deep to go when dumping arrays, via V, X, and x commands. For example:

```
perldb@monkey> perl -d -e 0
<...truncated output...>
  DB<1> @array = ('a'..'e')
  DB<2> x \@array
0  ARRAY(0x828e794)
   0  'a'
   1  'b'
   2  'c'
   3  'd'
   4  'e'
```

```
    DB<3> o arraydepth=2
          arrayDepth = '2'
    DB<4> x \@array
0 ARRAY(0x828e794)
    0 'a'
    1 'b'
    ....
    DB<5>
```

See also compactDump.

AutoTrace

Toggles tracing

The AutoTrace option sets tracing on or off. Setting this option to
true also sets $DB::trace and may be set in a couple of ways:

- Via the environment variable PERLDB_OPTS:

  ```
  perldb@monkey> PERLDB_OPTS='AutoTrace' perl -d ...
  <...truncated output...>
    DB<1> o AutoTrace?
          AutoTrace = '1'
    DB<2>
  ```

- As a toggle from within the debugger:

  ```
  perldb@monkey> perl -d -e 0
  <...truncated output...>
    DB<1> o AutoTrace?
          AutoTrace = '0'
    DB<2> t
  Trace = on
    DB<3> o AutoTrace?
          AutoTrace = '1'
    DB<4
  ```

See also $DB::trace in "Debugger Variables" and t in "Motion."

---

compactDump

Compacts dump variables

The compactDump variable compacts dump variables, when
dumping via V, X, and x. Using this option tends to place output
all on one line, which is useful for certain data structures. For
example:

```
perldb@monkey> perl -d -e 0
<...truncated output...>
  DB<1> %hash = ('this' = 'that', 'and' => 'so on')>
  DB<2> x \%hash
0 HASH(0x828e83c)
    'and' => 'so on'
    'this' => 'that'
```

```
  DB<3> o compactDump
        compactDump = '479'
  DB<4> x \%hash
0  HASH(0x828e83c)
    'and' => 'so on', 'this' => 'that'
  DB<5>
```

See also arrayDepth.

dieLevel   Toggles stacktrace at die

If the dieLevel option is set to 0, 1 or 2, the debugger prints out a
stacktrace when the running program dies. The default is 1.

Read the warning notes in the *perldebug* manpage about how
__DIE__ handler is unceremoniously modified if dieLevel is 2
or above.

See also signalLevel and warnLevel.

DumpDBFiles   Dumps debugged files

When the Boolean DumpDBFiles option is true, the debugger
dumps debugged files when dumping hashes via V, X, and x. The
default is 0 (false).

If DumpDBFiles is set, the complete file of the debugged file arrays
is printed, including all the files in %INC:

```
perldb@monkey> perl -d -e 0
<...truncated output...>
  DB<1> X
$/ = '
'
FileHandle(stderr) => fileno(2)
    'ABRT' => undef
<...truncated output...>
$^W = 0
FileHandle(STDERR) => fileno(2)
```

Although a lone X produces fairly voluminous output, setting
DumpDBFiles tends to produce more, even when constrained by a
pattern match, as the entire file(s) is displayed:

```
  DB<2> o DumpDBFiles
        DumpDBFiles = '1'
  DB<3> | X ~.*warnings.*
    $_</usr/local/lib/perl5/5.8.0/warnings.pm = '/usr/local/lib...
    @_</usr/local/lib/perl5/5.8.0/warnings.pm = (
  0  empty slot
```

```
 1    ' '
 2    '# !!!!!!!   DO NOT EDIT THIS FILE   !!!!!!! '
 3    '# This file was created by warnings.pl '
 4    '# Any changes made here will be lost.  '
 5    '# '
 6    ' '
 7    'package warnings; '
 <...truncated output...>
47    '           vec($warnings::DeadBits{\'all\'}, $warnings::LA...
48    '         } '
49    '} '
50    ' '
51    '1 ; '
  )
DB<4>
```

dumpDepth

Depth for dumping hashes

The dumpDepth option specifies how deep to go when dumping hashes via V, X, and x. This option is introduced in 5.8.0:

```
perldb@monkey> perl -d -e 0
<...truncated output...>
  DB<1> %hash = ('this'=>{'that'=>{'and'=>{'so'=>{'on'}}}})>
  DB<2> x \%hash
0  HASH(0x828e794)
   'this' => HASH(0x828e62c)
      'that' => HASH(0x828e65c)
         'and' => HASH(0x828e68c)
            'so' => HASH(0x80fa3a4)
               'on' => undef
  DB<3> o dumpDepth=3
         dumpDepth = '3'
  DB<4> x \%hash
0  HASH(0x831dfb0)
   'this' => HASH(0x831e0a0)
      'that' => HASH(0x831e10c)
  DB<5>
```

dumpPackages

Dumps symbol tables

The dumpPackages option specifies whether to dump the symbol tables while dumping hashes via V, X, and x.

Note that the regex constraint via V appears to be unreliable, as can be seen from the following example. When constrained by the .*mypkg.* regex, the following example still manages to return the FileHandle variables:

```
perldb@monkey> perl -d -e 0
<...truncated output...>
```

```
  DB<1> $mypkg::var='xxx'
  DB<2> o dumpPackages
        DumpPackages = '1'
  DB<3> V ~.*mypkg.*
$/ = '
'
    %mypkg:: = (
    'var' => *mypkg::var
)
<...truncated output...>
$^W = 0
FileHandle(STDERR) => fileno(2)
  DB<4>
```

DumpReused   Dumps data from reused addresses

The DumpReused option dumps the data held at the reused
addresses while dumping hashes via V, X, and x, instead of using
the space-saving REUSED_ADDRESS marker:

```
perldb@monkey> perl -d -e o
<...truncated output...>
  DB<1> $mypkg::var='xxx'
  DB<1> %hash = ('this'=>'that','mine'=>'yours')
  DB<2> $h_ref = { 'once'=>\%hash, 'twice'=>\%hash }
  DB<3> x $h_ref
0  HASH(0x831e130)
   'once' => HASH(0x831dfb0)
      'mine' => 'yours'
      'this' => 'that'
   'twice' => HASH(0x831dfb0)
      -> REUSED_ADDRESS
  DB<4> o DumpReused
        DumpReused = '1'
  DB<5> x $h_ref
0  HASH(0x831e130)
   'once' => HASH(0x831dfb0)
      'mine' => 'yours'
      'this' => 'that'
   'twice' => HASH(0x831dfb0)
      'mine' => 'yours'
      'this' => 'that'
  DB<6>
```

The debugger goes into an infinite loop if DumpReused is set and the
data structure you dump includes a self-referential element.

frame   Controls tracing on entering and exiting subroutines

The frame option controls the amount of tracing information
generated when entering and exiting subroutines.

See MaxTraceLen in "Quick Reference" for controlling the length of the arguments printed:

```
perldb@monkey> perl -d -e 0
<...truncated output...>
  DB<1> sub isachar { return $_[0] =~ /^[a-z]+$/i ? 'Y' : 'N' }
  DB<2> sub isanum  { return $_[0] =~ /^\d+$/    ? 'Y' : 'N' }
  DB<3> print join('-', isachar('xxx'), isanum('123'))."\n"
  Y-Y
```

After you have set up the program, look at these examples.

frame=0 gives a plain stack trace:

```
DB<4> o frame?
      frame = '0'
DB<5> t print join('-', isachar('xxx'), isanum('123'))."\n"
  main::((eval 10)[/usr/local/lib/perl5/5.8.0/perl5db.pl:17]:3):
  3:      print join('-', isachar('xxx'), isanum('123'))."\n";
  main::isachar((eval 8)[/usr/local/lib/perl5/5.8.0/perl5db.pl:
17]:2):
  2:      sub isachar { return $_[0] =~ /^[a-z]+$/i ? 'Y' : 'Y'
};
  main::isanum((eval 9)[/usr/local/lib/perl5/5.8.0/perl5db.pl:
17]:2):
  2:      sub isanum  { return $_[0] =~ /^\d+$/      ? 'Y' : 'N'
};
  Y-Y
```

frame=2 indicates entering and exiting of the subroutines:

```
DB<6> o f=2
      frame = '2'
DB<7> !5
  t print join('-', isachar('xxx'), isanum('123'))."\n" 3:
print join('-', isachar('xxx'), isanum('123'))."\n";
  entering main::isachar
  2:      sub isachar { return $_[0] =~ /^[a-z]+$/i ? 'Y' : 'N'
};
  exited main::isachar
  entering main::isanum
  2:      sub isanum  { return $_[0] =~ /^\d+$/      ? 'Y' : 'N'
};
  exited main::isanum
  Y-Y
```

frame=4 prints arguments and context:

```
DB<8> o f=4
      frame = '4'
DB<9> !5                    # <- repeat command no. 5
  t print join('-', isachar('xxx'), isanum('123'))."\n"
  3:      print join('-', isachar('xxx'), isanum('123'))."\n";
  in  @=main::isachar('xxx') from (eval 18)[/usr/local/lib/
perl5/5.8.0/perl5db.pl:17]:3
```

```
    2:     sub isachar { return $_[0] =~ /^[a-z]+$/i ? 'Y' : 'N'
};
  in  @=main::isanum(123) from (eval 18)[/usr/local/lib/perl5/5.
8.0/perl5db.pl:17]:3
    2:     sub isanum  { return $_[0] =~ /^\d+$/     ? 'Y' : 'N'
};
  Y-Y
```

frame=8 prints tied and referenced variables (may be buggy):

```
DB<10> o f=8
       frame = '8'
DB<11> t  print join('-', isachar(['xxx']), isanum([123]))."\n"
  3:        print join('-', isachar(['xxx']), isanum([123]))."\
n";
  entering main::isachar
    2:     sub isachar { return $_[0] =~ /^[a-z]+$/i ? 'Y' : 'N'
};
  entering main::isanum
    2:     sub isanum  { return $_[0] =~ /^\d+$/     ? 'Y' : 'N'
};
  N-N
```

frame=16 prints the return values from subroutines (similar to r
when PrintRet=1):

```
DB<12> o f=16
       frame = '16'
DB<13> !5
  t  print join('-', isachar('xxx'), isanum('123'))."\n"
  3:        print join('-', isachar('xxx'), isanum('123'))."\n";
  entering main::isachar
    2:     sub isachar { return $_[0] =~ /^[a-z]+$/i ? 'N' : 'N'
};
  list context return from main::isachar:
  0  'Y'
  entering main::isanum
    2:     sub isanum  { return $_[0] =~ /^\d+$/     ? 'Y' . 'N'
};
  list context return from main::isanum:
  0  'Y'
  Y
DB<14>
```

---

globPrint   Toggles printing of globs

The globPrint option specifies whether to print the contents of
globs via V, X, and x:

```
perldb@monkey> perl -d -e 0
<...truncated output...>
  DB<1> $x = 'x xx xxx'
  DB<2> @x = qw(x xx xxx)
```

The default is 0, in which case the debugger simply prints out that there is a variable with that name:

```
DB<3> o globPrint?
     globPrint = '0'
DB<4> x *x
  0 *main::x
```

When globPrint is set, each separate value is distinctly dumped:

```
DB<5> o globPrint
     globPrint = '1'
DB<6> x *x
  0 *main::x
    ${*main::x} = 'x xx xxx'
    @{*main::x} = (
       0  'x'
       1  'xx'
       2  'xxx'
    )
DB<6>
```

highbit
Toggles whether to quote octal characters

The highbit option specifies whether to quote all octal characters between \200 and \377.

See also quote and undefPrint.

inhibit_exit
Inhibits debugger exit

The inhibit_exit option controls whether the debugger quits at the end of the program or continues to run even after the program is ended. Standard behavior is to enable a restart, reusing currently set options, breakpoints, watch variables, etc. If inhibit_exit is set to 0, the debugger itself quits at the end of the program run, and control is returned to the calling process:

```
perldb@monkey> perl -d -e 0
<...truncated output...>
 DB<1> c
Debugged program terminated.  Use q to quit or R to restart,
  use O inhibit_exit to avoid stopping after program
termination,
  h q, h R or h O to get additional info.
 DB<1>
```

At this point you are still in the debugger environment at the end of your session and you can either quit or, if we wished to retain our history and actions for example, restart.

Alternatively, if inhibit_exit is set to 0, you just fall right off the end of the program:

```
perldb@monkey> perl -d -e 0
<...truncated output...>
  DB<1> o inhibit_exit=0
          inhibit_exit = '0'
  DB<2> c
perldb@monkey>
```

LineInfo   Outputs line information

The LineInfo option specifies where to send information that informs the programmer where she is in the code, including line numbers, the code about to be executed, breakpoint and action listings, etc. This information is typically sent to STDOUT, but you can reassign it to a file or a pipe with the LineInfo option.

If you assign LineInfo to a file, you can then *tail -f* this file in another window to track the program's execution. For example, suppose you assign LineInfo to *./db.out*:

```
perldb@monkey> perl -d linecounter.pl ^.*\s*mat input_file
<...truncated output...>
main::(linecounter.pl:8):       my @args = @ARGV;
  DB<1> o LineInfo=db.out
              LineInfo = 'db.out'
  DB<2>
```

From now on, the information about where you are in the code is sent to the *db.out* file. You can type merrily away without seeing very much, unless we look in *db.out*:

```
  DB<2> n
  DB<2> n
  DB<2> n
  DB<2> c
    2           the second line of the mat
Debugged program terminated.  Use q to quit or R to restart,
  use O inhibit_exit to avoid stopping after program
termination,
  h q, h R or h O to get additional info.
  DB<2> q
perldb@monkey>
```

Now if you display the contents of *db.out*, you can see all the useful information you are missing:

```
perldb@monkey> cat db.out
main::(linecounter.pl:11):my $help = grep(/^-h(elp)*$/i, @args);
main::(linecounter.pl:12):       if ($help) {
```

```
main::(linecounter.pl:17):         my $verbose = grep(/^-
v(erbose)*$/i, @args);
perldb@monkey>
```

This is how *vi, emacs, ddd*, etc. interact with the Perl debugger: capturing the feedback and presenting it in their own frames or windows.

---

maxTraceLen   Sets the maximum length of trace information

The maxTraceLen option specifies the maximum length of the subroutine arguments description string that should be printed when frame=4 is set. The default value for maxTraceLen is 400 characters.

To see this in effect, create and call a small subroutine with a long list of arguments:

```
perldb@monkey> perl -d -e 0
<...truncated output...>
  DB<1> sub call { print scalar(@_)." args\n" }
  DB<2> o frame=4
        frame = '4'
  DB<3> &call(1..50)
in  @=main::call(1, 2, 3, 4, 5, 6, 7, 8, 9, 10, 11, 12, 13, 14,
15, 16, 17, 18, 19, 20, 21, 22, 23, 24, 25, 26, 27, 28, 29, 30,
31, 32, 33, 34, 35, 36, 37, 38, 39, 40, 41, 42, 43, 44, 45, 46,
47, 48, 49, 50)
from
(eval 6)[/usr/local/lib/perl5/5.8.0/perl5db.pl:17]:2
50 args
  DB<4>
```

Then set maxTraceLen to a small number and call it again to see the difference:

```
  DB<4> o maxTraceLen=15
        maxTraceLen = '15'
  DB<5> !3
&call(1..50)
in  @=main::call(1, 2, 3, 4,... from (eval 7)[/usr/local/lib/
perl5/5.8.0/perl5db.pl:17]:2
50 args
  DB<6>
```

NonStop   Executes program without stopping

If the NonStop startup option is set, the program runs without interaction, with no need to type c to continue.

Note that $DB::single or $DB::signal still interrupts a running program even if NonStop has been set earlier.

NonStop must be set at initialization time. This means that if it is set within a debugger session with the o command, it won't take effect until the session is restarted:

```
perldb@monkey> perl -d -e 'print "Hello World\n"'
<...truncated output...>
main::(-e:1):   print "Hello World\n"
  DB<1> o NonStop
Too late to set up NonStop mode, enabled on next 'R'!
        NonStop = '1'
  DB<2>
```

Now restart the debugger session:

```
  DB<2> R
Warning: some settings and command-line options may be lost!
Hello World

perldb@monkey>
```

As a startup option, NonStop is frequently set in a *.perldb* file. It is typically used with the LineInfo option to send output to a file.

See also TTY and noTTY.

---

noTTY   Do not attach to a TTY

The noTTY option is a startup option that tells the debugger to not attach to a TTY. If noTTY is non-zero, the debugger enters NonStop mode automatically until interrupted (by $DB::signal, for example), at which point it uses the option specified in TTY. The default value for noTTY is 0.

The proper functionality of this option relies on the Term:: Rendezvous module.

See also LineInfo and TTY

---

ornaments   Adjust the appearance of the command line

The ornaments option affects the appearance of the command line. Its arguments can be either 0, 1, or a *termcap* code. See Term:: ReadLine for more information.

For example, you can query to see the default settings:

```
perldb@monkey> perl -d -e o
<...truncated output...>
```

```
main::(-e:1):    0
  DB<1> o orna?
             ornaments = 'us,ue,md,me'
  DB<2>
```

Then set reverse video and bold as attributes:

```
DB<2> o orna=mr,md
           ornaments = 'mr,md'
DB<3>
```

Use 1 to restore the defaults:

```
DB<3> o orna=1
           ornaments = 'us,ue,md,me'
DB<4>
```

---

pager   Specifies a pager for piped commands

The pager option defines which pager is used for piped
commands, and for the man and perldoc commands. The default
value is taken from $ENV{PAGER}.

See "Shell and Debugger Commands" for more on the | command
and "Help and Quitting" for more on the man and perldoc
commands.

In this example, set pager to return 3 lines of output on each
iteration:

```
perldb@monkey> perl -d -e 0
<...truncated output...>
  DB<1> o pager?
        pager = '|less'
  DB<2> o pager='more -3'
        pager = '|more -3'
  DB<3> |h h
Help is currently only available for the new 580 CommandSet,
if you really want old behaviour, presumably you know what
--More--
you're doing ?-)

T               Stack trace.
--More--
s [expr]        Single step [in expr].
n [expr]        Next, steps over subroutine calls [in expr].
<CR>            Repeat last n or s command.
--More--
```

quote Specifies how to quote strings

The quote option determines how to quote strings. Possible attributes are the default auto, ', and ". For example, first set up a variable to inspect and dump it to see the default behavior:

```
perldb@monkey> perl -d -e 0
<...truncated output...>
  DB<1> %hash = qw(this that)
  DB<2> x \%hash
0  HASH(0x831e0dc)
   'this' => 'that'
  DB<3>
```

Then change the default ' to " and dump the variable again:

```
  DB<3> o quote="\""
        quote = '"'
  DB<4> !2
x \%hash
0  HASH(0x831e0dc)
   "this" => "that"
  DB<5>
```

See also highbit and undefprint.

PrintRet Specifies whether to print return values from subroutines

The PrintRet option specifies whether to print the return value from subroutines to DB::OUT when using the r command. The default value is 0.

For example, place the following code in a file called *printret.pl*:

```
for (1..3) {
    my $var = call($_);
}

sub call {
    $DB::signal=1;
    return $_[0];
}
```

Then call the example with the debugger and use c to continue to the breakpoint set by DB::single above:

```
perldb@monkey> perl -d -e printret.pl
<...truncated output...>
  DB<1> c
main::call(runit:7):            return $_[0];
  DB<2>
```

Set printRet=0 to ensure nothing is printed and use r to return from the subroutine:

```
    DB<2> o printRet=0
        PrintRet = '0'
    DB<3> r
main::(runit:1):        for (1..3) {
    DB<4>
```

Continue once more and set printRet=1 this time to see what is printed when you return from the subroutine:

```
    DB<4> c
main::call(runit:7):            return $_[0];
    DB<5> o printRet=1
        PrintRet = '1'
    DB<6> r
scalar context return from main::call: 2
main::(runit:1):        for (1..3) {
    DB<7>
```

See also r in "Motion."

---

recallCommand   Defines the command for repeating a previous command

The recallCommand option specifies the character used to recall a previous command from the history list. The default is !. The command to run a shell command is set to !!, and this can lead to some confusion, so the debugger provides the recallCommand and shellBang options to redefine one (or both).

For example, try !pwd and the problem is clear. By forgetting to double the exclamation point, the debugger thinks you're trying to run a history command and generates an error:

```
    DB<3> !pwd
No such command!
    DB<3>
```

The caret character ^ is a reasonable alternative for "go up" the history list. So set recallCommand=^:

```
    DB<4> o recallCommand=^
        recallCommand = '^'
    DB<5> !pwd
/home/perldb
    DB<6> ^
/home/perldb
    DB<7>
```

For other ways of remapping inconvenient commands, see also = in "Shell and Debugger Commands."

ReadLine

ReadLine is a Boolean startup-only option for debugging modules that use Term::ReadLine themselves. The default is 1.

See Term::ReadLine for more information.

RemotePort

RemotePort is a startup-only option that sets the machine and port to attach to for a possibly remote debugging session, given in host:port format.

shellBang

The shellBang option specifies which character to use for a shell or host command. The default value of ! shares the same character with recallCommand. For example:

```
perldb@monkey> perl -d -e 0
<...truncated output...>
  DB<1> o shellBang=~
ShellBang = '~'
  DB<3> ~pwd
/home/perldb
  DB<4>
```

Redefining the recallCommand may be a better solution.

signalLevel

If the signalLevel option is set to 1 or higher, the debugger prints out a stacktrace if the running program is interrupted by a signal. Read the warning notes in the *perldebug* manpage about how __SIG__ handlers are modified unceremoniously if signalLevel is 2 or above. The default is 1.

See also dieLevel and warnLevel.

tkRunning

The tkRunning option enables the Devel::ptkdb to prompt for input. The default value is either N/A or /dev/tty. This option is similar to ReadLine: it is used by a specific module or program to capture input, and is otherwise not very useful.

The TTY option specifies the device to use for debugging I/O and is primarily used by various programs to gain control of the debugger for themselves—for example when interacting with editors (*vi*, *emacs*, etc.) or debuggers (*ddd*, *komodo*, etc.). The default is /dev/tty.

See also noTTY and LineInfo in "Quick Reference."

undefPrint   Whether to print undef for undefined values

The undefPrint option specifies whether to print undef for an undefined value. The default value is 1.

For example, dump a list with an undefined value within it:

```
perldb@monkey> perl -d -e 0
<...truncated output...>
  DB<1> @arr = ('one', undef, 'three')
  DB<2> x \@arr
0   ARRAY(0x831e084)
   0   'one'
   1   undef
   2   'three'
  DB<3>
```

Then redefine the undefPrint variable and dump the list again:

```
  DB<3> o undefPrint=0
        undefPrint = '0'
  DB<4> !2
x \@arr
0   ARRAY(0x831e084)
   0   'one'
   1   ''
   2   'three'
  DB<5>
```

See also highbit and quote in "Quick Reference."

UsageOnly   Print memory usage stats

The UsageOnly option specifies whether to print basic memory usage statistics for any package given to the V or X commands. Not all variables are included (such as lexicals in a module's scope), but UsageOnly can still give you an idea of the amount of memory being used.

See also PERL_DEBUG_MSTATS in "Debugger Variables."

For example, load the CGI.pm module with a use statement to examine its package variables:

```
perldb@monkey> perl -d -e 0
<...truncated output...>
  DB<1> o UsageOnly?
        UsageOnly = 'N/A'
  DB<2> use CGI
  DB<3> V CGI
$DEFAULT_DTD = ARRAY(0x83fb530)
   0  '-//W3C//DTD HTML 4.01 Transitional//EN'
   1  'http://www.w3.org/TR/html4/loose.dtd'
$revision = '$Id: options.pod,v 1.44 2003/10/13 08:50:50 perl...
$PRIVATE_TEMPFILES = 0
$::ISA::CACHE:: = 1160
<...truncated output...>
$DISABLE_UPLOADS = 0
  DB<4>
```

Then set UsageOnly=1 and display the variables for CGI again. This time, the debugger prints several variables with memory information:

```
  DB<4> o UsageOnly
        UsageOnly = '1'
  DB<5> V CGI
%::ISA::CACHE:: = 5 items (keys: 23; values: 0; total: 23 bytes)
%Util:: = 17 items (keys: 128; values: 332; total: 460 bytes)
%EXPORT_TAGS = 12 items (keys: 74; values: 192; total: 266
bytes)
String space: 67212 bytes in 91 strings.
Grand total = 67961 bytes (1 level deep) + overhead.
  DB<6>
```

A grand total of 67K. Not a lot in these days of gigabytes of memory (and given the amount of work CGI does), but interesting all the same.

---

windowSize   Number of lines of code displayed

The windowSize option specifies the number of lines of code to display when using v, l, etc. The default value for windowSize is 10. You may want to modify the display of the code because of the size of the window in which you are viewing, or because of the visual structure of the code itself.

For example, load the Config.pm module from the %INC array:

```
perldb@monkey> perl -d -e 0
<...truncated output...>
```

```
DB<1> f Config
Choosing /usr/local/lib/perl5/5.8.0/i586-linux/Config.pm
matching `Config':
1       package Config;
2:      use Exporter ();
3:      @EXPORT = qw(%Config);
4:      @EXPORT_OK = qw(myconfig config_sh config_vars);
5
6       # Define our own import method to avoid pulling in th...
7       sub import {
8:        my $pkg = shift;
9:        @_ = @EXPORT unless @_;
10:       my @func = grep {$_ ne '%Config'} @_;
    DB<2>
```

Now you can redefine windowSize to the value 3 and see how this affects the amount of information shown:

```
    DB<2> o windowSize=3
          windowSize = '3'
    DB<3> l
11:       local $Exporter::ExportLevel = 1;
12:       Exporter::import('Config', @func) if @func;
13:       return if @func == @_;
    DB<3>
```

Prior to 5.8.0, the window size has to be given as an argument to each v and l command.

veryCompact

Dumps hashes compactly

The Boolean veryCompact option specifies how to dump hashes when using the x command. It is not recommended to use this option, as it appears to be buggy. See compactDump for an alternative.

To demonstrate the veryCompact option, first build a structure and dump it using the x command:

```
    perldb@monkey> perl -d -e 0
    <...truncated output...>
      DB<1> %hash = ('this' => 'that', 'and' => 'so on')
      DB<2> x \%hash
    0  HASH(0x83fd27c)
       'and' => 'so on'
       'this' => 'that'
      DB<3>
```

Now set veryCompact to 1 and redo the command to view the result:

```
    DB<3> o veryCompact
          veryCompact = '1'
```

```
    DB<4> !2
x \%hash
0
    DB<5>
```

Note that if used with an array, the output may be just as surprising:

```
    DB<5> @arr = (1..30)
    DB<6> x \@arr
0
    DB<7>
```

If this weren't bad enough, when given a more complicated data structure to dump, the behavior just gets worse:

```
    DB<7> %hash = ('this'=>{'that'=>{'and'=>{'so'=>'on'}}})
    DB<8> x \%hash
0  HASH(0x831dfb0)
    'this' => HASH(0x831e10c)
      'that' => HASH(0x831df80)
        'and' => HASH(0x817e448)
          'so' => 'on'
    DB<9> !2
x \%hash
0  HASH(0x831dfb0)
    'this' => HASH(0x831e10c)
      'that' => HASH(0x831df80)
        'and' => Not an ARRAY reference at /usr/local/lib/p...
          dumpvar::DumpElem('HASH(0x817e448)',12,-5) called at /u...
          dumpvar::unwrap('HASH(0x831df80)',9,-4) called at /usr/...
          <..truncated output...>
          main::dumpValue('ARRAY(0x831df20)',-1) called at /usr/...
          DB::dumpit('GLOB(0x81844fc)','ARRAY(0x831df20)') called...
          DB::eval called at /usr/local/lib/perl5/5.8.0/perl5db.p...
          DB::DB called at -e line 1
Debugged program terminated.  Use q to quit or R to restart,
  use O inhibit_exit to avoid stopping after program
termination,
    h q, h R or h O to get additional info.
    DB<9>
```

Basically, just use compactDump instead.

---

warnLevel
Prints a stacktrace if the program prints a warning

If the warnLevel option is set to 0, 1, or higher, the debugger generates a stacktrace if the running program prints a warning. The default value for warnLevel is 1.

Read the warning notes in the *perldebug* manpage about how __WARN__ handlers is modified unceremoniously if warnLevel is 2 or above. Allegedly, the 3 options dieLevel, signalLevel, and warnLevel all drastically affect the relevant handlers and tracing mechanisms during program execution, although I remain unconvinced about this.

To demonstrate the warnLevel option, first put the following code into a file named *levels.pl*:

```perl
$SIG{__WARN__} = sub {
  print "xxx warning inside the handler xxx\n";
};

$SIG{__DIE__} = sub {
  print "xxx dieing inside the handler xxx\n";
  die "*** dieing here ***";
};

call();

sub call {
  moan();
}

sub moan {
  print("xxx printing xxx\n");
  warn("xxx warning xxx");
  die("xxx dieing xxx");
};
```

To see the initial values of all three (die|signal|warn)Level handlers without having to type this in all the time, place the following code in *.perldb*:

```perl
sub afterinit {
  push(@DB::typeahead, 'o warn?', 'o die?', 'o sig?');
}
```

Now set the dieLevel, signalLevel, and warnLevel options in various combinations on the command line, and run the following command:

```
perldb@monkey>PERLDB_OPTS="die=0warn=0 sig=0"perl -d levels.pl
<...truncated output...>
main::(levels.pl:4):    };
auto(-3)  DB<1> o warn?
             warnLevel = '0'
auto(-2)  DB<2> o die?
             dieLevel = '0'
auto(-1)  DB<3> o sig?
          signalLevel = '0'
  DB<4>
```

Having noted the initial settings for reference, now use c to continue execution and observe the behavior:

```
DB<4> c
xxx printing xxx
xxx warning inside the handler xxx
xxx dieing inside the handler xxx
*** dieing here *** at levels.pl line 8.
Debugged program terminated.  Use q to quit or R to restart,
  use O inhibit_exit to avoid stopping after program
termination,
  h q, h R or h O to get additional info.
DB<4>
```

Now modify the settings on the command line:

```
perldb@monkey>PERLDB_OPTS="die=2 warn=0 sig=1" perl -d levels.pl
<...truncated output...>
main::(levels.pl:4):    };
auto(-3)  DB<1> o warn?
            warnLevel = '0'
auto(-2)  DB<2> o die?
            dieLevel = '2'
auto(-1)  DB<3> o sig?
          signalLevel = '1'
  DB<4>
```

Note that they have indeed changed and use c once more:

```
DB<4> c
xxx printing xxx
xxx warning inside the handler xxx
xxx dieing inside the handler xxx
*** dieing here *** at levels.pl line 8.
Debugged program terminated.  Use q to quit or R to restart,
  use O inhibit_exit to avoid stopping after program
termination,
  h q, h R or h O to get additional info.
DB<4>
```

There is no discernible change in behavior despite what is described in the documentation.

See also dieLevel and signalLevel.

DB and Devel Namespaces

This section describes the namespaces and hooks that are available in Perl for the debugger to use. It covers:

- Where the debugger library is stored
- In which order the options and the *rc* file are parsed
- The DB:: and the Devel:: namespaces
- How to use the perl -D switch

The debugger is not an integral part of the Perl interpreter. Instead, the debugger is a separate program that is implemented in the *lib/perl5db.pl* file in the Perl distribution. Perl provides certain runtime and compiletime hooks, enabled by running Perl with the -d command line switch.

The advantage of the debugger is that, because it is itself written in Perl, it can be customized or replaced as needed.

The debugger runs in the DB namespace:

```
package DB;
```

See DB::DB and PERL5DB in "Debugger Variables."

When Perl is called with the -d:module flag, it calls a module in the Devel namespace. This is the most common way of interacting with the hooks Perl provides.

Some of this is explained below. For more information on this theme, see the *perlrun* manpages.

Runtime Sequence

The sequence of events when the standard Perl debugger starts up are as follows:

1. Initialization

   Load the appropriate debugger code. This is where you can create your own debugger to run, via the BEGIN {require $debugger_filename} statement. See PERL5DB in "Debugger Variables."

2. *.perldb*

   This is the *rc* file for the Perl debugger, where certain options are parsed. This file (*.perldb* or *perldb.ini*) is looked for at startup in the current directory and then in the users' home directory on Unix. See the *.perldb* entry in "Shell and Debugger Commands."

3. PERLDB_OPTS

   The PERLDB_OPTS environment variable is used to pass particular options to the debugger at startup. It is also possible to place an explicit call to DB::parse_options(...) in the *rc* file *.perldb* refered to above. See PERLDB_OPTS in "Debugger Variables."

4. DB::afterinit()

   If defined, the DB::afterinit() subroutine is called after debugger initialization. This subroutine is conditionally called after all files have been compiled and the debugger greeting has been printed. See *.perldb* in "Shell and Debugger Commands."

   The DB::parse_options() function parses a PERLDB_OPTS options line. It may be called from within DB::afterinit. See *.perldb*.

   During execution of DB::afterinit(), commands may be pushed onto the DB::typeahead array before the debugger session runs.

5. DB::postponed()

   After each file is compiled, but before it has been executed, the DB::postponed() function is called (if it exists). It is called with a glob like this:

   ```
   DB::postponed(*{"_<$filename"})
   ```

   See *perldebguts* for more info on this and DB::postponed("subname").

DB::DB()

Before each line is executed, the DB::DB() function is called. This is the heart of the debugger, where each command is parsed and run in the context of the line about to be executed.

This is where it is decided whether the program is at a breakpoint and whether there is something to do, such as an action or watch expression, pre-prompt or post-prompt command, etc.

You can write your own handler by redefining the standard DB::DB() subroutine:

```
perldb@monkey> PERL5DB='BEGIN {sub DB::DB{print "."}}' perl -d
-e 'print "hi\n"; print "hi2\n"'
.hi
.hi2
perldb@monkey>
```

For more useful examples, see the PERL5DB variable in "Debugger Variables."

DB::sub ()

Before each subroutine, function or method is called, the DB::sub() function is called instead, wrapping up the call so that the debugger has control over it and the arguments it returns.

See *perldebguts*.

Devel Namespace (-d)

Perl has a special namespace, Devel, that holds most of the debugging and program development modules. As syntactic sugar, -d can nearly be thought of as meaning Devel:: as well as enabling the runtime hooks described below and in "Debugger Variables."

Whenever Perl is called with the -d switch and a colon (:) is followed by a bareword, it looks inside the Devel:: namespace for the given module.

For example, place the following minimal code in a file called
DebugModule.pm in the *Devel* directory:

```
package DebugModule;

sub DB::DB {
  # do nothing
}

1;
```

See DB::DB above for how to make this subroutine do something useful.

Now the following code calls Devel::DebugModule on the *helloworld.pl* program:

```
perldb@monkey> perl -d:DebugModule helloworld.pl
Hello World
perldb@monkey>
```

Module options may be passed in after an equals sign (=),
with multiple options being separated by commas (not
spaces), just as with the -M switch:

```
perldb@monkey> perl -d:DebugModule=opt1,opt2,opt3,etc
helloworld.pl
Hello World
perldb@monkey>
```

Note that this does not mean that all Devel::* modules work
directly with the -d switch. If the module does not implement the DB::DB function, perl -d:*modulename* fails with the
appropriate error message.

Place this code into the file *DebugDuff.pm* in the *Devel*
directory:

```
package DebugModule;

sub DB::not_a_DB_subroutine {
  # do nothing
}

1;
```

Now run this command line and Perl complains about the missing subroutine:

```
perldb@monkey> perl -d:DebugDuff helloworld.pl
No DB::DB routine defined at helloworld.pl line 1.
perldb@monkey>
```

The code above is not the same as calling the Devel::* module with -M, which uses the module but not run it. In this case Perl does not implicitly expect a DB::DB subroutine.

In the following example, the DebugModule is loaded and the program *prog* is run. The debugger is not invoked at all:

```
perldb@monkey> perl -MDevel::DebugModule helloworld.pl
Hello World
perldb@monkey>
```

For more info on Perl's command-line switches, see the *perlrun* manpage.

Useful Modules

Here is a short summary of modules that you may find useful for debugging, troubleshooting, and general program development. The following is a selective listing of useful modules in the Devel namespace:

Devel::Cover
> Reports how much code your program executes, of the code you have written.

Devel::DProf
> Reports on the execution time of your code. It is one of the most useful modules to learn how to use, and then use.

Devel::Leak
> Finds memory leaks.

Devel::Peek
> Shows you what Perl *really* thinks of your variables.

Devel::SmallProf

> Similar to Devel::DProf but with a smaller footprint, and less likely to give the dreaded "segment violation" message.

Devel::Size

> Shows the amount of memory Perl allocates to your variables.

Devel::Timer

> Handy alternative to the Benchmark module for timing chunks of code.

Devel::Trace

> Similar to using AutoTrace, but can be used programatically instead of directly via the debugger.

In addition to the many other very useful Devel::* modules available on the CPAN, the following modules are also noteworthy. Note that one or two are here just to demonstrate what can be done with a little imagination, and to increase the fun factor while hunting for bugs:

Acme::Bleach

> To paraphrase Lord Nelson: "What bugs? I see no bugs!"

B::Deparse

> See what Perl *really* thinks of your program.

B::Xref

> Displays all defined variables and subroutines, etc.

Benchmark

> Times chunks of code at a high resolution.

Symbol::Approx::Sub

> Never, ever, use this module in production—it is deranged and the pod is worth reading!

Tie::Watch

> Watches variables as they are accessed (read, modified, or deleted).

This implements similar functionality to creating watch expressions in the debugger, but programatically rather than interactively.

-DDEBUGGING

If your Perl has been compiled with -DDEBUGGING, there are a number of switches you can use on the command line with the -D flag. For how to compile with this flag, see *INSTALL* in your Perl source distribution.

Debugging a regular expression

You can debug a regular expression on the command line like this:

```
perldb@monkey> perl -Dr -e '/^pe(a)*rl$/i'
Compiling REx `^pe(a)*rl$'
size 17 Got 140 bytes for offset annotations.
first at 2
rarest char
 at 0
   1: BOL(2)
   2: EXACTF <pe>(4)
   4: CURLYN[1] {0,32767}(14)
   6:   NOTHING(8)
   8:   EXACTF <a>(0)
  12:   WHILEM(0)
  13: NOTHING(14)
  14: EXACTF <rl>(16)
  16: EOL(17)
  17: END(0)
floating ''$ at 4..2147483647 (checking floating) stclass
'EXACTF <pe>' anchored(BOL) minlen 4
Offsets: [17]
        1[1] 2[2] 0[0] 7[1] 0[0] 4[1] 0[0] 5[1] 0[0] 6[1] 0[0]
7[0] 7[0] 8[2] 0[0] 10[1] 11[0]
Omitting $' $& $' support.

EXECUTING...

Freeing REx: '`"^pe(a)*rl$"'
```

For info on what all this means, see the *perldbguts* manpage.

Execution tree

perl -Dtls prints an execution tree:

```
perldb@monkey> perl -Dtls helloworld.pl
(helloworld.pl:5)  ENTER scope 2 at toke.c:1027
(helloworld.pl:5)  LEAVE scope 2 at toke.c:1129
    =>
(helloworld.pl:5)  null
    =>
(helloworld.pl:5)  const(PV("Hello World\12"\0))
    =>  PV("Hello World\12"\0)
(helloworld.pl:5)  stringify
(helloworld.pl:8)  ENTER scope 2 at op.c:6985
(helloworld.pl:7)  LEAVE scope 2 at op.c:7333
(helloworld.pl:0)  LEAVE scope 1 at perl.c:1551
(helloworld.pl:0)  ENTER scope 1 at perl.c:1559
(helloworld.pl:0)  Setting up jumplevel bffff35c, was 816cb40

EXECUTING...

    =>
(helloworld.pl:0)  enter
(helloworld.pl:0)  ENTER scope 2 at pp_hot.c:1624
Entering block 0, type BLOCK
    =>
(helloworld.pl:0)  nextstate
    =>
(helloworld.pl:5)  pushmark
    =>  *
(helloworld.pl:5)  const(PV("Hello World\12"\0))
    =>  *  PV("Hello World\12"\0)
(helloworld.pl:5)  print
Hello World
    =>  SV_YES
(helloworld.pl:5)  nextstate
    =>
(helloworld.pl:7)  const(IV(0))
    =>  IV(0)
(helloworld.pl:7)  exit
Leaving block 0, type BLOCK
(helloworld.pl:0)  LEAVE scope 2 at perl.c:4150
(helloworld.pl:0)  Setting up jumplevel bffff354, was 816cb40
(helloworld.pl:0)  LEAVE scope 1 at perl.c:430
perldb@monkey>
```

For more info on how to use -D see the *perlrun* manpage.

References

The following reference materials are available for the debugger:

- The documentation library that comes with Perl accessed through *perldoc*
- Books on debugging and interesting or related material
- Online references to debugging with Perl
- GUIs and text editors that make it easier to debug Perl programs

perldoc

The *pod* directory is a great source of information about Perl. Browsing through it will give you ideas for how to solve your next coding problem and invariably help you write better Perl programs.

Use *perldoc* on the shell command line or the debugger command line. In the shell:

```
perldb@monkey> perldoc docfile
```

Or within the debugger:

```
DB<4> man docfile
```

To find the path to the *perldoc* installation on your system, use the following command:

```
perldb@monkey> perldoc -l perl
/usr/local/lib/perl5/5.8.0/pod/perl.pod
```

The following is a selective list of some of the documentation files that are distributed with Perl:

perltoc
> The table of contents for all the Perl documentation distributed with the source.

perlfaq

> The Frequently Asked Questions index for Perl. You'd be amazed how many people have already come across (and solved) your unique problem, as well as nearly everybody else's.

perldebug

> The definitive reference to the Perl debugger.

perldebtut

> A lightweight tutorial in the usage of the Perl debugger.

perldebguts

> A descent into the internal functionality of the debugger.

perlrun

> Command line arguments and how they affect your Perl program.

perldiag

> Verbose diagnostics for errors. Everyone should read this and take a look at *splain*.

Books

The following is a list of books on aspects of debugging with Perl and other recommended reading:

Programming Perl by Larry Wall, Tom Christiansen,
and Jon Orwant (O'Reilly)

> The essential Perl reference, known as the Camel Book or the Perl Bible or the Blue Book, depending on your perspective. It includes a short section on using the debugger.

Perl Debugged by Peter Scott and Ed Wright (Addison Wesley)

> Covers a lot of useful ground for general debugging techniques, and more importantly, presents coding practices to prevent the need for so much debugging in the first place.

Extreme Programming by Kent Beck (Addison Wesley)

A damn good read, expounding the virtues of frequent code releases, peer reviews for code, and as much testing as you can squeeze in.

Testing is something that most programmers appear to shy away from with ridiculous regularity. This book, and liberal usage of make test, help focus the mind wonderfully.

The Psychology of Computer Programming by
Gerald M. Weinberg (Dorset House)

As the author says (in 1971), "It's amazing how little one generation of programmers seem to learn from the mistakes of their forbears."

Safeware: System Safety and Computers by Nancy Leveson
(Addison Wesley)

An eye-opener about what goes wrong in some of the big projects you hear about. Contains some interesting examples of dreadful design (i.e., sequences such as *A B D C*) by people who are paid to know better.

Mastering Regular Expressions by Jeffrey E. F. Friedl
(O'Reilly)

Everything you ever wanted to know about regexes, and a lot you never will.

Chess Fundamentals by Jose Capablanca (Cadogan books)

Thinking about chess can lead to insights about the interdependencies of different chunks of a program, and how one small thing, probably a forgotten pawn in the corner, can seriously affect the outcome of a mission critical application.

The Pleasure of Finding Things Out by Richard Feynmann
(Penguin)

Keep your mind open and have fun—particularly while dealing with difficult problems.

URLs

The following are URLs and online references for debugging with Perl:

http://www.perl.com
> The Perl home.

http://www.perl.org
> The other Perl home.

http://debugger.perl.org
> The debugging with Perl site.

Debugger mailing list
> The mailing list for debugging with Perl. To subscribe:
>
> *debugger-subscribe@perl.org*
>
> An archive is available at:
>
> *http://www.mail-archive.com/debugger@perl.org*
>
> Other Perl mailing lists are available at:
>
> *http://lists.perl.org/*

Perl bugs
> If you think you've found a bug in Perl, this is the place to go to see what happened to it:
>
> *http://bugs.perl.org/*

CPAN
> The Comprehensive Perl Archive Network (CPAN), home to all self-respecting modules:
>
> *http://cpan.perl.org*

Perl source
> The latest Perl source is always retrievable from *perl.com* and *perl.org* and the CPAN.

Perlmonks
> The source of much activity and many inspirations:
>
> *http://www.perlmonks.org*

YAPC

These people build conferences for like-minded people and help bring the community together in tangible places around the world:

> *http://www.yapc.org*
> *http://www.yapc.org/Europe*

perl5db notes

In addition to *perldebug*, *perldebtut*, and *perldebguts*, documentation enhanced by Joe McMahon comes with the debugger itself, explaining some of how it actually works:

> *http://ibiblio.org/mcmahon/debugger.html*

perl5db.pl

Last but not least, if you want the most up-to-date version of the Perl debugger, you can get it here:

> *http://www.activestate.com/perlsource/get?lib/perl5db.pl*

Online Articles

The following is a selection of online articles relating to the debugger, either useful by themselves or as pointers to other links:

perlmonks—Perl debugger articles
    http://www.perlmonks.org/index.pl?node=debugger+perl

perlmonth
    *http://www.perlmonth.com/perlmonth/issue2/mod_perl.
    html*

drdobbs
    http://www.ddj.com/documents/s=1498/ddj0108pl/

devshed—Using the Perl debugger
    http://www.devshed.com/Server_Side/Perl/PerlDebugger

grin—Perl debugger intro
    http://www.grin.net/~mirthles/web/perldb_talk.html

slashdot—Debugger related articles
    http://slashdot.org/search.pl?query=debugger

History

Perl has always had a debugger, since the language started life at the hands of Larry Wall in 1987. Originally the syntax was:

```
perldb@monkey> perldb prog progargs
```

It was in Perl Version 3 (1989) that Larry gave the debugger a big workover and the familiar, and current, -d usage came about:

```
perldb@monkey> perl -d prog
```

The Perl debugger is now a work of many hands. Tom Christiansen and Ilya Zakharevich in particular have gotten their hands the dirtiest in developing the debugger. Gurusamy Sarathy has built an OO API to the debugger, which may be the base of the Perl 6 debugger. Currently the relevant module is DB.pm in the Perl distribution.

GUIs—Graphical User Interfaces

There are a number of Graphical User Interface (GUI) Perl debuggers available, for different platforms. The nice thing about a GUI debugger is it gives separate windows for command input, source code, and output. When placing the mouse cursor over a variable, it displays the value. Essentially, GUI debuggers add an ease-of-use layer to the existing functionality.

Some of these interface to the existing *perl5db.pl* debugger, while others have created their own interpretation of it. Therefore, the command sets and APIs differ somewhat from one to another, although the general principles remain similar.

Debuggers

The following is a very narrow selection of what is available:

ddd

Runs on Unix as a front end to *gdb*. This is an alternative to Devel::ptkdb if you happen not to have the appropriate Perl/Tk modules installed:

```
perldb@monkey> ddd perl prog args
```

See *man ddd* for more info.

komodo

Runs on Windows and Linux. The *komodo* debugger is an integral part of the full Integrated Developer Environment (IDE), which can be bought from ActiveState. Note the Windows version does not run on DOS.

ptkdb

The classic Perl debugger GUI for all Unix flavors, and works just as well on Windows. The easiest way to install this is via the CPAN:

```
perldb@monkey> perl -MCPAN -e 'install(Tk,Devel::ptkdb)'
```

Then to run the GUI:

```
perldb@monkey> perl -d:ptkdb prog
```

A neat trick to debug CGI programs is to create a BEGIN block in which you set your environment variable DISPLAY to wherever (that is, on which target machine) you want the *ptkdb* window to appear:

```
BEGIN { $ENV{DISPLAY} = '192.168.0.7' }
```

pvdb

A favorite that uses *vi* as the front end to the debugger:

http://www.perl.com/language/misc/pvdb

oradb

A Perl command-line interface to the Oracle-supplied PL/SQL debugger. It enables a programmer to step through a stored procedure or PL/SQL package, in a similar manner to using the Perl debugger. Download from:

http://cpan.perl.org/RFOLEY/Oracle::Debug

For more GUI, IDE, and debugger ideas, see *perlfaq3*.

Text Editors

For text editors with debugging support, you will need a programmer's editor. One of the following may be suitable:

vim
> For Unix, Windows, and the Mac OS, available from:
>> *http://www.vim.org*

emacs
> For Unix, Windows, and Mac OS X, available from:
>> *http://www.gnu.org/software/emacs*

ultraedit
> For Windows, available from:
>> *http://www.ultraedit.com*

bbedit
> For the Mac OS, available from:
>> *http://www.bbedit.com*

For more text editor and IDE ideas, see *perlfaq3*.

Quick Reference

Actions

	Create	Delete
Action	a [line] command [condition]	A (line|*)
Breakpoint	b [line [condition]] compile subname | [postpone] subname [condition] load filename	B (line|*)
Watch	w [expr]	W (expr|*)
List	L [a|b|w]	

Pre-Post Prompt Commands

	Create	Append	Delete
Pre-debugger	< [expr|?]	<< expr	< *
Post-debugger	> [expr|?]	>> expr	> *
Pre-perl	{ [expr|?]	{{ expr	{ *

Motion

Continue	c [line|sub]
Next	n [expr]
Return	r
Step (into)	s [expr]
Trace	T
Trace toggle	t [expr]

Code Listings

View filename	f filename
List code	l [min+incr|min-max|line|subname|$var]
View code	v [line]
Repos. display	.
Continue	-
Search forward	/regex[/]
Search back	?regex[?]

Examining Data	
Print	p expr
Methods	m (expr|class)
Module versions	M
Subroutines	S [[!] ~pattern]
Vars	V [pkg [vars]]
Dump	x [maxdepth] expr
Vars curr pkg	X [vars]
Vars lexical	y [level [vars]]
Commands	
Pager	|dbcmd [args]
Shell command	!! cmd
Eval	any perl command
Run filename	source filename
Restart	R
Alias	= [alias value]
History list	H [-number]
History redo	! [[-]number] | [pattern]
Documentation	
Help	h [cmd] | h h
Manual pages	man manpage | perldoc
Quit	q
Options	
Options	[opt|opt?|opt=val|opt="val"]

Index

We'd like to hear your suggestions for improving our indexes. Send email to
index@oreilly.com.

W

W command, 60
w command, 59
–W command-line option, 11
–w command-line option, 11
$^W special variable, 11
Wall, Larry, 3, 119, 123
warnings
  diagnostics and, 11
  splain program and, 13
  turning on/off, 11
warnLevel option, 107
watchpoints
  command quick
    reference, 126
  deleting, 60
  listing, 61
  setting, 59
  source command and, 73
  vs. Tie::Watch module, 115

Weinberg, Gerald M., 120
windowSize option, 105
Wright, Ed, 119

X

X command, 33
x command, 17, 21, 31–33
–X command-line option, 11

Y

y command, 34
YAPC (Yet Another Perl
    Conference), 122

Z

Zakharevich, Ilya, 123

Related Titles Available from O'Reilly

Perl

O'REILLY®

Our books are available at most retail and online bookstores.
To order direct: 1-800-998-9938 • *order@oreilly.com* • *www.oreilly.com*
Online editions of most O'Reilly titles are available at *safari.oreilly.com*

Keep in touch with O'Reilly

1. Download examples from our books

To find example files for a book, go to:
www.oreilly.com/catalog

select the book, and follow the "Examples" link.

2. Register your O'Reilly books

Register your book at *register.oreilly.com*

Why register your books? Once you've registered your O'Reilly books you can:

- Win O'Reilly books, T-shirts or discount coupons in our monthly drawing.
- Get special offers available only to registered O'Reilly customers.
- Get catalogs announcing new books (US and UK only).
- Get email notification of new editions of the O'Reilly books you own.

3. Join our email lists

Sign up to get topic-specific email announcements of new books and conferences, special offers, and O'Reilly Network technology newsletters at:
elists.oreilly.com

It's easy to customize your free elists subscription so you'll get exactly the O'Reilly news you want.

4. Get the latest news, tips, and tools
www.oreilly.com

- "Top 100 Sites on the Web"—PC Magazine
- CIO Magazine's Web Business 50 Awards

Our web site contains a library of comprehensive product information (including book excerpts and tables of contents), downloadable software, background articles, interviews with technology leaders, links to relevant sites, book cover art, and more.

5. Work for O'Reilly

Check out our web site for current employment opportunities:
jobs.oreilly.com

6. Contact us

O'Reilly & Associates, Inc.
1005 Gravenstein Hwy North
Sebastopol, CA 95472 USA

TEL: 707-827-7000 or 800-998-9938
(6am to 5pm PST)

FAX: 707-829-0104

order@oreilly.com
For answers to problems regarding your order or our products.
To place a book order online, visit:
www.oreilly.com/order_new

catalog@oreilly.com
To request a copy of our latest catalog.

booktech@oreilly.com
For book content technical questions or corrections.

corporate@oreilly.com
For educational, library, government, and corporate sales.

proposals@oreilly.com
To submit new book proposals to our editors and product managers.

international@oreilly.com
For information about our international distributors or translation queries. For a list of our distributors outside of North America check out:
international.oreilly.com/distributors.html

adoption@oreilly.com
For information about academic use of O'Reilly books, visit:
academic.oreilly.com

O'REILLY®

Our books are available at most retail and online bookstores.
To order direct: 1-800-998-9938 • *order@oreilly.com* • *www.oreilly.com*
Online editions of most O'Reilly titles are available at *safari.oreilly.com*